MR. NEW YORK

MR. NEW YORK

Lew Rudin and His Love for the City

Seymour P. Lachman

Foreword by President Bill Clinton

excelsior editions

An imprint of State University of New York Press
www.sunypress.edu

Cover photo of Lew Rudin by Yousuf Karsh courtesy of the Rudin family.

Printed in the United States of America

Excelsior Editions is an imprint of State University of New York Press

For information, contact State University of New York Press, Albany, NY
www.sunypress.edu

Production by Ryan Morris
Marketing by Michael Campochiaro

Library of Congress Cataloging-in-Publication Data
Lachman, Seymour.
Mr. New York : Lew Rudin and his love for the city / Seymour P. Lachman ; foreword by President Bill Clinton.
pages cm. — (Excelsior editions)
Includes bibliographical references and index.
ISBN 978-1-4384-5197-8 (hardcover : alk. paper) 1. Rudin, Lewis, 1927–2001 2. Real estate business—New York (State)—New York. 3. Business and politics—New York (State)—New York. I. Title. II. Title: Mister New York.
HD268.N5L33 2014
974.7'1043092—dc23
[B]

2013027108

10 9 8 7 6 5 4 3 2 1

For the People of the City of New York

Contents

Foreword by President Bill Clinton *ix*
Preface *xi*
Acknowledgments *xiii*

1. "Take Care of Our City" 1
2. Family Roots 13
3. Entree to Politics and Policy 31
4. Birth of the Association for a Better New York 45
5. The Film and Television Industry Comes of Age in New York City 57
6. The Looming New York City Fiscal Crisis 61
7. Prepayment of Property Taxes, and the Road Back to Prosperity 69
8. New York City Marathon 81
9. International Tennis Becomes Synonymous with New York 85
10. Protecting Local and State Tax Deductions 91
11. A Living Landmark 99

Notes *103*
Index *111*

Foreword

President Bill Clinton

I met Lew Rudin when I was still living in Arkansas, before my time in the White House and long before New York became my adopted home state.

In the mid-'80s, Lew and I had teamed up to fight President Reagan's proposal to cut state and local income tax deductibility. Our successful campaign led to a wonderful friendship—between the two of us and between our families.

When we first met, it was clear to me that Lew was a New Yorker to his very core. He measured his own successes and failures by how the city was doing: if the city thrived, he thrived; if the city faltered, he was on the phone with a handful of people—politicians, developers, and likeminded residents—figuring out the best way to put it back on top.

Lew was friendly with lawmakers at every level. He contributed frequently and generously to efforts on both sides of the aisle, supporting whomever he believed would best serve his city and state. Politicians and citizens alike knew that an endorsement from Lew carried a lot of weight, and I was grateful to have his support when I ran for president.

When I won re-election in 1996, Lew was one of the first to send flowers and call with his best wishes. His kindness meant a lot, but I also knew it carried an unspoken message: I had done right by New Yorkers. The Brady Handgun Violence Prevention Act of 1993 and the Violent Crime Control and Law Enforcement Act of 1994 had added one hundred thousand new police officers to the streets across America, legislated an assault weapons ban, and kept handguns away from more than five hundred thousand felons and fugitives; and thanks to our highly contested economic plan, interest rates had dropped, the deficit was moving toward a balanced budget and surpluses, and millions more were working and moving out of poverty into the middle class. Lew let me know he saw the results on the streets of New York. And for him, results counted more than good intentions.

He took the same approach when it came to his generous giving. In the early 1970s, when New York's luster was starting to fade, Lew founded the Association for a Better New York to promote the well-being of the city and state. I've been delighted to support ABNY throughout the years, and was proud when, last winter, Chelsea took the ABNY stage to moderate a panel on child welfare. It all started when Lew and I connected thirty years ago.

His life is a gift that keeps on giving, through the work, generosity, and friendships of his family and through the inspirational example he set for other successful people: if you do well, you must also do good. Because of Lew, New York is stronger, safer, and cleaner. And because of Lew, my life and the lives of countless others are richer.

Preface

Throughout my professional career, as a teacher and a public official, I have focused my interest on the role of government in improving the lives of its citizens. My doctoral research dealt with Federal Aid to Education legislation, which took one hundred years of legislative commitment and compromise before it was passed by Congress and signed into law by President Lyndon Johnson. In the 1970s, I was a member and then president of the New York City Board of Education, which was created after the bitter and divisive teachers strike of 1968. The newly appointed board and the elected community school boards were part of the decentralization of the city's public schools. This initiative was designed to empower community members and parents, based on the theory that community involvement would enhance student achievement. I wrote about the successes and problems of these efforts as ethnic politics emerged and became a key factor in New York City's public education system. Years later, as an elected member of the New York State Senate, I became aware of the limited power of most legislators. Locally elected by their communities, they often were unable to represent their constituents' interests as decisions were made by "three men in a room." Several years ago, I studied New York Governor Hugh

L. Carey's role in harnessing the "best and the brightest" in government, business, labor, and the civic community to save the City of New York from bankruptcy in the 1970s. My analysis clearly demonstrated what strong leadership can achieve when its power is used to ensure that the public and private sectors work together for the greater good.

With this portrait of the life and times of Lew Rudin, I see the issue from a different perspective. Lew Rudin was a private citizen; he held no office and had no official title, but his love, commitment, and belief in the viability of the city motivated him to use his talents and resources to make New York a better place for us all, and earned him the nickname, "Mr. New York."

Acknowledgments

This book would not have been possible without the major assistance of Robert Polner, senior fellow at the Hugh L. Carey Institute for Government Reform. It could also not have been written without the complete cooperation of Lew Rudin's children, Bill Rudin and Beth Rudin DeWoody; his wife, Rachel; and his brother, Jack Rudin; as well as the entire Rudin Family.

The author is also grateful to Richard Guarasci, the president of Wagner College on Staten Island, New York, and the staff of the college's Hugh L. Carey Institute for Government Reform, especially Suzanne D'Amato, Megan Marin, and Marc Rivlin.

Most especially, the author gratefully appreciates and wishes to thank President Bill Clinton for taking time out of a very busy schedule to write a foreword.

Many thanks go out to the individuals who agreed to interviews and allowed us the opportunity to learn about Lew Rudin from their own extensive recollections, observations, and insights: Michelle Adams, Lori Barclay, Martin Bregman, Pamela Delaney, Mayor David Dinkins, Public Advocate Betsy Gotbaum, George Gowen, Mary Holloway, Secretary of State Henry Kissinger, Mayor Ed Koch, Jay Kriegel, Kenneth Langone, George Lence, Vicki Lurie, Michael McKee, the Hon.

Milton Mollen, Sen. Manfred Ohrenstein, Lt. Governor Richard Ravitch, Ambassador Felix Rohatyn, Howard Rubenstein, Beth Rudin DeWoody, Bill Rudin, Jack Rudin, Ophelia Rudin, Rachel Rudin, Susan Rudin, David Specter, Jonathan Tisch, Randi Weingarten, and Deputy Mayor John Zuccotti.

The Rudin archives, which the Rudin family maintains in the offices of Rudin Management Company, Inc., were extremely helpful. This is also true of the archives maintained in the office of the Association for a Better New York, whose current executive director, Jennifer M. Hensley, and deputy director, Jordan Isenstadt, were most helpful as well. Lois Towe, Bill Rudin's executive assistant, did a fine job with the process of coordinating our research and interviews, and her efforts were of great assistance. Finally, and most importantly, to my wife Susan without whom nothing in my life of any significance could have been accomplished.

1
"Take Care of Our City"

When Lew Rudin died in September 2001, after a battle with cancer, his pronounced civic passion was highlighted over and again at his funeral service at Central Synagogue on the Upper East Side of Manhattan. The service also underscored the extent to which the Rudin family and their concentric circles of friends had cherished his warm and caring nature. That he died less than two weeks after terrorists struck down New York's World Trade Center made the loss for many of the attendees even more poignant.[1]

The 9/11 attacks on New York City, which destroyed thousands of lives while threatening to topple the city from its preeminent position as the financial capital of the world, had left Rudin's hometown reeling from shock, grief, and anger, and made many fearful of a repeat attack. Ground Zero in Manhattan was a smoldering pile of wreckage, swarming with firefighters and others searching for survivors and human remains. Ever watchful after 9/11, U.S. fighter jets streaked through the skies. National Guard members directed traffic. Police in riot helmets toted high-powered weapons; others guarded transit terminals and tourist destinations. New Yorkers of every class and ethnic grouping felt a keen sense of vulnerability and kinship in ways they had rarely experienced.

In his active and fruitful years, Lew Rudin had moved others to act on behalf of his greatest love—the City of New York. His ideas, zeal, and bullishness in battling for the city's advancement were well known. During the 1970s fiscal crisis, for example, he and a few of his friends in the real estate and tourism sectors detected early, and responded to, serious threats to the long-term economic competitiveness of the city.[2] They partnered with local and state government to fight the rising tide of troubles. At his core, Rudin believed that what was harmful to the business climate was also not good for the city as a whole.

But now he was gone, and to the people in the historic synagogue who testified to his character and had been touched by his generosity and unremitting sense of purpose, and who were at times struck by his usually unassuming manner, his death seemed, for the moment at least, almost impossible to imagine.

Known widely as "Mr. New York," Rudin was an ardent defender of cities in an era of urban decline and suburbanization. He was, above all, a New York City stalwart when the city was, especially to many conservatives around the country, the poster child for everything wrong with government and the nation—whether it was overcrowded schools, aging transportation systems, or racial tensions and riots, among many other serious challenges. Many will remember Rudin for handing out tiny golden apples to almost everyone he met when the Big Apple was struggling to pull itself out of periodic recessions and crime waves, pinning the ornaments on taxi drivers, teachers and ordinary citizens. Along with the golden apples, he freely offered advice to elected officials, from borough presidents and mayors, to governors, U.S. senators and even the president of the United States. Some will recall his assistance in popularizing the commercially devised, state-promoted "I Love New York" slogan, or the "New York is a Great College Town" banner that the Koch administration promoted in the late 1970s and early 1980s. Such spirited efforts represented a strong and principled counterstatement to the widespread reputation of the city in those years as dangerous, and dying, and were characteristic of Rudin's civic influence and impact.

Lew Rudin was seventy-four and had suffered from glaucoma for most of his life, making him almost blind at his death on September 20, 2001, though he had become surprisingly adept at recognizing and distinguishing the voices of close friends.[3] In his last days, at his own request, and after talking it over with his family, he left the hospital to return home. His son Bill wondered how or whether he would deliver the news of the 9/11 attacks to his extremely fragile father. But his dad, never out of touch with the galloping pulse of New York City developments, had already heard of the Trade Center attacks. While for many people, the waning days of one's life is a time to draw the curtain of privacy, Lew Rudin was always a public-minded figure, trying to connect with others to the very end, and he wanted to see his friends and those who mattered to him one last time.

The ebb and flow of visitors to the Upper East Side penthouse apartment he shared with his wife, Rachel, included Hillary Rodham Clinton, New York's new junior senator. "He held her tightly by the arm and said, 'Take care of our city,' " Bill recalled.[4]

So it was that Rudin was eulogized with genuine affection at Central Synagogue, the Moorish, twin-turreted house of worship on Lexington Avenue at East Fifty-Fifth Street where he had been a congregant. The synagogue, within walking distance of both his home and his office and where he had also served as a trustee, exudes history and permanence, a national landmark so designated in 1975. It offered a sorely needed moment of contemplation to the hundreds who came to pay their respects, and not surprisingly, they were a veritable *Who's Who* of New York movers-and-shakers in culture, politics, business, labor, medicine, education. Some attendees headed nonprofits that aided the poor and sick, which the Rudin family had supported generously and quietly over the years. Others were recognizable from sports and entertainment. There were also some who were not known for their influence or wealth—secretaries, doormen, and long-time Rudin Management tenants who knew Lew as both a prominent person and someone who remembered and knew the names of his employees as well as their spouses or children, who telephoned or sent a handwritten note when someone in their family took ill, and treated people of all stations of life with courtesy and respect.

He treated the metropolis, too, as if it were a friend or family member, dropping everything and charging into often-contentious issues, believing he had a duty to contribute his ideas and if necessary his money to aid New York when it was in trouble. A tall man, usually wearing aviator glasses, his occasional bluntness and gruff demeanor only belied his "pussycat" nature, said a close friend. Another said he did not pick fights or harbor grudges. He practiced persistence, but his basic approach was to negotiate civilly rather than to confront with threats or blame. To the very end, he looked for ways to make a positive contribution, and enlist like-minded citizens in his latest cause.

Weeks before his death, in fact, an ailing Rudin managed to attend the re-dedication of the same historic synagogue where his funeral service would be held. He arrived at the re-dedication ceremony in a wheelchair, wearing an oxygen mask, and joined fellow congregants in marking its reconstruction from a devastating 1998 fire, a project for which he had donated much financial support.

If for that cause very late in his life and so many others before it Rudin acted as a kind of community organizer, albeit in one of the wealthiest zip codes in the country, then those who gathered for his funeral were his committed allies. Speakers recalled him in various ways as a man of action with firm persuasions, a builder, a salesman, a numbers guy, a landlord, a golfer, a devoted son, husband, father, grandfather and brother, and someone committed to the Jewish people and Israel and, above all, New Yorkers of all creeds, races, and religions. Former president Bill Clinton said during the funeral service that Lewis once introduced him to an audience "by saying I was younger than him and better looking than him, but he was richer. When I spoke to him last week he said I wasn't president anymore, I was older than I used to be—and he was still richer than me! Being in Lew Rudin's life was like being in a magnetic field. You were always being pulled somewhere whether you wanted to go or not."

Rudin's daughter, Beth Rudin DeWoody, who, like her brother Bill, now holds a senior position in the family business along with overseeing the family's three philanthropic foundations, said her father was going to be buried with an upholstered pillow on which was emblazoned a favorite phrase, "No Good Deed Goes Unpunished." She joked that when she was born, a friend told her father to buy his baby girl some blocks. "So he bought me Fifty-First Street and Fifty-Second Street,"[5] she said, brushing her tears.

The actor Sidney Poitier said Rudin, a close friend and golfing partner, had called him the previous Monday and asked him to say "goodbye" on his behalf to the City of New York.

"Rest easy, Lew," Poitier said softly. "The City of New York has your love wrapped around its heart."[6]

The words that brought the crowd to their feet were spoken by then-Governor George Pataki. Referring to 9/11, Pataki said, "We will rebuild our city. We have no choice because this is Lew Rudin's New York."[7]

Draped by an American flag, the casket was carried out of the sanctuary by pallbearers, and his grandson Michael carried Lew's gold clubs while caddies held other golf clubs aloft, the gift of Deepdale Country Club at Lake Success in Nassau County, N.Y., where Rudin loved to tee up. Golf was the sport he enjoyed most, next to schmoozing.[8]

"His memorial service was like a funeral for a Jewish Kennedy," read a column in *New York* magazine a year later.[9]

Who, then, was this gravelly voiced, third-generation leader of a major Manhattan real estate family and New York power broker who attracted so many friends—and in a city where the real estate business is sometimes cutthroat and litigious, and where some people accord their landlord the same level of warmth they might have for a uniformed officer giving them a parking ticket?

Yes, he was a good man who supported a lot of worthy causes. But why did he matter, and why might the story of his notable civic involvement still matter?

What does the example of a successful businessman's unusual commitment to his city, state, and country say at a time when the nation is divided deeply by ideology, race, and region, an era when small armies of lobbyists and special interests dominate national and state legislatures, and modest regulations risk distorting elections and legislative processes? In a time when cynicism runs rampant about government at virtually all levels, Wall Street, and the "one percent" of the nation, what did Rudin do to become a force of progress?

Lew Rudin believed, firstly, that business, labor, and government could and should partner in the public interest, and his life was filled with examples of acting on this instinct and impulse. In fact, he lived them out and invariably found a way to reconcile competing and even hostile interests rather than riding roughshod over those which at first may have appeared irreconcilable with his own. Rarely did he let much more than an hour or two pass without phoning or meeting others to refresh the bonds of friendship. He never seemed to care what people's politics were—some, in fact, had no idea if he was a Republican or Democrat, liberal or conservative. He just liked being in continuous touch with those who were trying to make an honest deal or a difference, and loved to know what was going on in their lives and happening all across town and down at City Hall. When there was a public problem—there were always plenty of them to go around—he sought to know whether he could help, and if so, how, and how soon.

A native of New York City, Rudin understood that sometimes he could develop more stimulating, interesting, and useful contacts simply by loitering at a single intersection in Manhattan—say, the corner of Fifty-Second Street and Park Avenue, where he liked to buy a hot dog from the street vendor—than anywhere else in the country. (In 2002, East Fifty-Second Street between Park and Lexington avenues was dedicated in Lew's memory as "Lew Rudin Way.") He appreciated the idea and power of "intersection" that his 24/7 city of doers and thinkers offered, and the value it brought to his personalized way of conducting business. He was interested in interacting with others all the time, given his tendency to consider diverse points of view. Once, he visited a political science class on Marxism at New York University to make the argument in favor of capitalism at the invitation of the professor, Bertell Ollman, a respected scholar, who viewed history and political economy through a lens of class conflict and struggle.[10] On several occasions, he went on television to debate leading advocates of local rent control and rent stabilization laws, the bane of New York City landlords.

"He was probably one of the most effective salesmen that there was," the late Walter Wriston, CEO of Citibank and one of the nation's most powerful bankers in the 1970s, once said, referring to Lew's relentless defense of and advocacy for the city during New York's financial troubles in the mid-1970s. "Bear in mind," Wriston went on, "when he was doing it nobody was buying."

It was in the 1970s that Rudin emerged as the public face of the New York real estate sector and became a compelling salesman for civic betterment when the city seemed to need outside help more than at any time since at least the Great Depression. In 1971, together with businessman Preston Robert Tisch, real estate executive Irving Schneider, banker Rexford Tompkins, real estate developer Charles Benenson, and publicist Howard Rubenstein, among others, Rudin helped found the Association for a Better New York, or ABNY, which endures to this day under Bill Rudin's leadership. After devising and pushing through a way for the cash-strapped city to collect property tax revenues from major property owners in the city earlier than scheduled, and thereby helped keep it out of bankruptcy, Lew Rudin, Howard Rubenstein, and other well-connected New York businessmen helped convince Democratic Party leaders to hold the party's nominating convention at Madison Square Garden in New York in the bicentennial year of 1976.

Presidents, governors, and mayors knew Lew by his first name, and U.S. senators and representatives almost always returned his calls. Leading politicians, presidential cabinet appointees, and business executives attended evening parties at his home as well as ABNY's prominent, usually packed breakfast forums. Former mayor Ed Koch put it this way in 2012: "There are families in every city that have nobility attached to them. The Wagner family is one of them. And the Rudin family is one, too. They take the position that the city is bigger than all of us and needs all of us to attend to its needs."[11]

"It wasn't just his wealth," said former New York City public advocate Betsy Gotbaum, who headed the Police Foundation of New York in the late 1970s, when Rudin was serving as a member of its board. "It was that he was involved in *everything,* and if he believed in what you were trying to accomplish, he would never turn you down." One issue that she vividly recalls was how helpful he was when she and others raised the topic of the need for bulletproof vests for New York City police officers.[12]

Lew's desire to stay connected to the most compelling and influential New Yorkers was also reflected by the interfaith rapport he and his brother Jack, his lifelong real estate partner, enjoyed with the Catholic Church of New York. Jack initiated and maintained meetings and a dialogue with successive Roman Catholic archbishops of New York. The ties started with John Cardinal O'Connor in the 1980s. Jack was so fond of Cardinal O'Connor that he went on to send a delivery of bagels and lox each and every Friday morning to St. Patrick's Cathedral for Cardinal O'Connor and his staff to enjoy.

According to Jack Rudin, his wife, Susan, and Lori Barclay, a Rudin Management vice president and Lew Rudin's assistant, the habit of providing a Friday morning breakfast to the reigning archbishop of New York continued with Cardinal O'Connor's successor, Edward Cardinal Egan, and most recently with Timothy Cardinal Dolan.[13] The family's ties to the church, though, stretched back to a previous generation, as Lew and Jack's father, Sam, had been friendly with Francis Joseph Cardinal Spellman.

Lew Rudin also annually held a party at the Regency Hotel to mark the end of Yom Kippur for 250 relatives and friends, regardless of their religion. He rented apartments and offices from his family's real estate portfolio to many former local, state, and federal public officials and high-level government appointees newly retired from their taxpayer-furnished homes, among them former mayors William O'Dwyer, Ed Koch, and David Dinkins. Lew, according to his son, never cared what office a politician held or what his record on any particular issue was when a current or former official was hunting for an apartment to rent. For Rudin, his company's assistance was a reflexive gesture of respect for those who had held public office, his son said.

In a similar gesture of respect, Rudin also attended the funeral of Henry Kissinger's father in 1982. The former secretary of state and advisor to presidents Richard Nixon and Gerald Ford recalled in an interview that Lew Rudin told him that he had read Louis Kissinger's obituary in the morning newspaper and just felt that he needed to show up and pay his respects. Kissinger noticed Rudin's presence at the funeral service and was moved. "I can't remember him ever asking me for anything," Kissinger said in response to an interviewer's question many years later, adding, "I thought of him as part of the solution, not as someone who needed to be placated, and as a great public servant."[14]

Rudin brought together former and current elected and appointed officials, Kissinger included, to speak at his ABNY's monthly morning forums, seating the more prominent ones at the head table, willfully oblivious to their sometimes intense rivalries or grudges of the moment. Rudin felt they could, and should, get along and work together for the good of the city, or at the very least be civil toward each other publicly.

The monthly ABNY gatherings began with one hundred or so attendees and grew to include hundreds more on a regular basis by the 1990s and into the twenty-first century, becoming a mandatory stop for politicians and others wishing to be seen and heard by New York's business and political elites and press. Among the many people taking the microphone at various times were George H. W. Bush and his son, George W. Bush, Bill Clinton, Gerald Ford, Ronald Reagan, Bob Dole, Ted Kennedy, Al Gore, Jack Kemp, and General Colin Powell, each one introduced with humor, breeziness, and warmth by the bespectacled "Mr. New York."

At one point, while Bill and Beth were youngsters, Rudin frequented the iconic East Side pub P. J. Clarke's on Sunday afternoons. Sometime the children were dropped off there by their mother, Gladyce, Lew's first wife, after religious school. They ate burgers and fries and listened politely in P. J. Clarke's, if not always able to comprehend fully the banter and laughter about real estate closings, local and state politics, and sports. Friends dropped by throughout the afternoon, knowing Rudin would be there, holding court in the same genial, unaffected way he came to emcee the ABNY power breakfasts.[15]

For all his usual informality, the developer was no-nonsense when he detected a slight against his hometown. He rarely passed up a chance to phone the *New York Times* or some other media outlet, large or small, to grouse about an article or a newscast he perceived as having placed New York in an unfair light. Responding to a 1990 newspaper column about a woman who left the city because of the cost of living, drug problems, and crime, Rudin fired off a letter to the editor urging her to return "to the Big Apple and help us solve not only New York's problems, but all of the social problems of this great country."[16]

2
Family Roots

Lewis Rudin was born on April 4, 1927, but the family's ties to New York date to his paternal grandfather, Louis Rudinsky, who arrived in Manhattan in 1883 after an ocean voyage from his ancestral home in eastern Poland.

Like many new immigrants, the young Rudinsky possessed only the coins in his pocket as he entered the New World at Castle Clinton in Battery Park, the predecessor to the great immigrant gateway on Ellis Island. As he stood alone on these alien shores, he would soon be met by relatives who could help him, especially his older brothers Harry and Joe, who were already working in the coat and suit business in Brooklyn.

After working at a string of jobs available to a newcomer who could barely speak English, Louis started a small business with his wife, Rachel, in the teeming, impoverished Lower East Side, the center of the Jewish immigrant community in rapidly industrializing America.

For millions of Jews as well numerous other religious and ethnic groups pouring out of Europe in the late nineteenth and early twentieth centuries, America and New York were, for all their hardships and disappointments there, a refuge. For the vast majority of East European Jews, it was an escape from violent state-sanctioned pogroms conducted by roving thugs, as well as a path out of poverty. Louis Rudinsky had been drafted into the Tsarist army at age fifteen. Depending on the time, his village, Valozhin, was considered part of Russia, Belarus, or Poland.

Like many other young men who resisted the Russian military draft and their government's wars, Louis saw America not only as a place where a Jew could practice or not practice his religion as he saw fit, without fear of persecution, but where he could also own property without limitation or fear of interference, as was sometimes the case in Tsarist Russia. He soon collected the travel papers needed to board a ship and was on his way from his family's ancestral home.

In 1890, seven years after arriving in America, Rudinsky and his wife opened their shop—a grocery on Chrystie Street. The first four of the Rudinsky's nine children would be born in a small apartment in the rear of the store where the family lived, including Lew and Jack's father, Samuel. The next five children arrived in a five-story walk-up on Manhattan's East Fifty-Fourth Street, the first piece of real estate Rudinsky ever purchased, in the early 1900s. Curiously, the ambitious immigrant had one of the richest men in America, John D. Rockefeller, to thank for his ownership of this impressive-sounding East Side address.

The story of this house purchase goes back to the turn of the century, when an oil price war raged between the biggest petroleum tycoons of the day, the news of which was all over the English and even the Yiddish newspapers of the city. The rivalry among the moguls saw each one lowering his prices to undercut the competition. The Rudinsky grocery sold a lot of kerosene, the lighting and heating fuel of the era. John D. Rockefeller of Standard Oil traveled up from Wall Street along Broadway, stopping and checking in with retailers to seek retailers' cooperation to keep his kerosene prices competitive and moving as quickly as possible off the shelves. One day his horse and buggy stopped at the Rudinsky store and the famous multimillionaire surprised the apron-wearing proprietor by walking in and introducing himself.

"Mister Rockefeller, I am honored to meet you," Rudinsky said in his Yiddish accent. Before the breathtaking encounter ended—"my grandfather's proudest moment," according to Jack Rudin[1]—the grocer got up enough courage to engage Rockefeller in polite conversation and asked him where he lived.

"I live on Fifty-Fourth Street," came Rockefeller's reply.

In 1905 a real estate broker named Joshua Cantowitz visited Rudinsky. Louis, ever restless in search of something better for himself and his family, had left the grocery and followed his brothers into the garment business. Cantowitz advised, "I know you wanted to buy a piece of real estate. There's a little apartment house, a five-story building, steam-heated, that might be right for you."

Where was this property, asked Rudinsky? Fifty-fourth Street, said the broker, who suggested Rudinsky go and have a look.

Louis, along with his brother Joseph, bought it, sight unseen.[2] "If it's good enough for Mister Rockefeller, it's good enough for me," he explained.

That a recent arrival could buy a home on the same street as the Rockefellers must have been almost unbelievable to Lew and Jack's grandparents, well beyond their most optimistic dreams about the possibilities of a safe and decent life for a Jewish immigrant. That the apartment was actually located more than three blocks east of Rockefeller's opulent and palatial home, economically a world away, hardly mattered to Rudinsky. He used his savings to buy the $4,000 house that had been built for the stablehands of the wealthy families living along bucolic Central Park.

In keeping with the basic freedoms America offered, Lew's grandfather established a small synagogue on the Lower East Side, which he named for his native village, Valozhin. He died in the early 1920s, before Lew was born, and Lew was named for him. Lew's grandmother Rachel lived until the mid-1940s. The house on Fifty-Fourth Street that grandfather Louis bought in 1905 was later joined by adjacent properties purchased by Lew's father, Sam, and his siblings, who turned all of these adjacent parcels into a thirty-two-story midtown commercial office building, 641 Lexington Avenue, soaring high into the sky, which the family still owns.

"It was based on a gut feeling they had," Lew, a student of the family history, told an interviewer who asked about his grandfather's original purchase of the home and the development of the site by a determined Sam Rudin. "Some people have a talent for music, some people have it for writing. My grandfather and my father had it for real estate."[3]

Sam Rudin indeed had what his two sons called an insatiable appetite to build buildings, an appetite that on only a few occasions exceeded his digestive ability. He founded Rudin Management in 1924, and both alone and later with the help of his sons built and managed twenty-three residential apartment buildings and fifteen commercial office buildings, nearly all located in midtown and lower Manhattan.

Sam's first business investment, however, was in the east Bronx.

He and his wife, May, a Harlem-born bookkeeper when they met, had by then purchased a modest and attractive home for their growing family to live in. It had a gently sloping roof line over a long row of windows facing front, and was located in the Throgs Neck section of the Bronx, then and now a leafy and attractive neighborhood. While awaiting a Pelham Line train one day in 1927, Sam peered downward from the elevated platform at Westchester Square and saw where he wanted to erect his first building. He and May and other members of their extended family pooled their funds and took out a bank loan to acquire and build, on the grounds of a lumber yard, a six-story house at 1400 Benson Street. The building remains part of the Rudin Management, Inc., portfolio.

By the time the nation's high-flying stock market collapsed in 1929 and the Great Depression set in intractably, Sam had taken out loans and purchased two other properties—elegant apartment houses on West Eighty-Sixth Street in Manhattan. At the end of the 1930s, as the economy began to improve and Europe was again at war, Rudin Management built another apartment building, at Ninetieth and Central Park West. But the family's building boom really took off after World War II, as veterans returned and started families, and the city government struggled to address a major shortage of decent and affordable housing. The Rudin portfolio would, by the twentieth century's end, come to include about a dozen new Manhattan apartment houses, with more than four thousand individual dwelling units in all, as well as more than a dozen major Manhattan office buildings.

Sam had no formal education in the construction business, as Lew once said of his father. After Townsend Harris High School, he attended City College but did not graduate because he had to take over his father's coat and suit business upon his death. "He was good at it, but he didn't like it at all," said Lew. "He knew how to manufacture coats and suits and said, well, it can't be too much different to build a building's foundation, to put the steel work on, and so on. So he learned. He hired a good architect and a good superintendent. He knew how to let out contracts from being in business. And he sold and rented the apartments. Then he got into office buildings."

Lewis adored his "pop," for whom he and his older and equally devoted brother, Jack, began working steadily after their completion of military service in World War II. Throughout their lives, and long after he had died, they loved talking about their father.

"He was a gentle man; he very rarely yelled," Lew said after his own children were grown and working for the company. "He had a tremendous way with people. There was a human touch with him. It didn't matter whether you were on the lowest end of the staff in a building or were the president of the bank. He knew how to handle you. He built up trust. When my father shook hands with bankers who had loaned him money, they knew they were going to get their money back."[4]

One friend of Lew's, the late municipal union advisor and negotiator Jack Bigel, noticed Rudin's genuine devotion to his father on numerous occasions. "One thing that did strike me was his constant reference to his family roots," Bigel once told an interviewer. "He and his brother Jack invariably would talk about their father at great lengths. When either of them talked about real estate taxes, they would eventually wind up by saying, 'As my father said…' They'd either wind up or start that way."[5]

In 1955, Sam Rudin and his family built their first commercial building, 415 Madison Avenue at Forty-Eighth Street. Additional commercial development soon followed including 641 Lexington Avenue (1964), 1 Battery Park Plaza (1971), 55 Broad St (1967) (the original headquarters of Goldman Sachs), and 345 Park Avenue (1969), which serves as the headquarters of Bristol-Myers Squibb and the National Football League in addition to housing the offices of Rudin Management.

In the late 1950s, the Rudins built a one million square foot office building at 80 Pine Street, which, while adjacent to the Wall Street financial district, was surrounded by old warehouses that served the waterfront. Due to its location, the project was "quite a gamble," Lew would recall. Costing about $3 million, this building proved difficult for the Rudins to rent out.

The problem was that the Pine Street address was considered too far from the heart of the financial district to attract established stock brokerages. "One broker said, 'You're on the wrong side of the tracks.' What tracks?" remembered Lew, who by then was working closely with his brother and father. But the Third Avenue el had once rumbled past the site along Pearl Street, en route to the Staten Island ferry slip. The area retained a somewhat gritty reputation.

If the established brokerages steered clear, the Pine Street building at least attracted a Big 10 accounting firm as well as an engineering company. Finally, a senior partner with a Wall Street brokerage firm broke ranks. Eschewing a lease in a Maiden Lane office building because the name "Maiden" didn't sound like a true financial address to his ears, whereas "Pine" did, he advised his real estate broker to rent from the Rudins.

After that, other brokerage houses felt comfortable enough to step beyond the invisible boundaries of the district, and Sam Rudin wasn't so much of an outsider anymore on Wall Street.

The change paid dividends later.

"Late in nineteen fifty-eight, I got a call from a friend in [a major bank]," Lew recalled. "'Don't get excited,' he told me, 'and please don't tell your father, but I'd like to know something about the base of your building, the rentable space.' Over time, we rented three hundred thousand square feet to [the bank], which gave us the opportunity to show the world that we had a viable product."

In the manner of many real estate companies, Rudin Management continued to depend on the instincts of its president and founder, Sam, rather than market research or hired consultants.

"We don't need marketing studies," Sam was once quoted in the *New York Times*, reflecting his belief in following one's own gut, rather than so-called experts, in the world of building and ownership. "When the time is right, we build."

Lew needed to exert a restraining influence on his father at times, and could effectively do so by the early 1960s. When the Rudin family was negotiating for the British government to relocate from space in Rockefeller Center to a new Rudin building on Third Avenue in 1963, Rockefeller Center demanded a $100,000 payment from the Rudins to let the British terminate the existing leases. It was a price Sam considered intolerable, in part given the inordinate wealth of the Rockefellers.

He was going to call David and Nelson Rockefeller and ask them 'What do you want this money for?'" remembered Lew. But the son steadied his father's emotions as he,

Jack, and Sam were heading over to close the deal, telling him the payment was just the cost of doing business. "'Gee pop, isn't this a wonderful country?'" Lew recalled saying, quickly adding the clincher: "'Here we are, walking over to Rockefeller Center, and the son of a Jewish immigrant is able to give the Rockefeller family one hundred thousand dollars. I mean isn't this a great country?' And he looked at me, and his whole attitude changed, just like that. He then became bigger than them; he was giving them a hundred thousand dollars."

An astute, hard-driven businessman, Sam worked six days a week. He was known as a shrewd observer of the real estate market, envisioning and investing in New York's postwar growth while nurturing an uncanny memory for every contact he ever made in every building he ever built and leases he signed. His sense of timing was not always dead-on, however—for whose could be, after all? He did not believe, in 1971, that the city's economic downturn was going to last long, and pushed ahead with an office project at 41 Madison Avenue, along with two more apartment houses. Yet by 1975, when the office building at 41 Madison was completed, the city recession was deeper and even more intractable. This major Rudin Management building was hard to fill because of the difficult financial times that brought New York City to the brink of bankruptcy.

Rare for him, Sam Rudin felt that he had overreached and miscalculated in a perhaps unredeemable way. Feeling bereft, he told his sons, "I ruined it for you boys."[6]

As a stopgap measure, the Rudins turned the building into the New York Merchandise Mart, a center for manufacturers and importers of home furnishings, giftware, and antiques, and so it remained. They held on and their prospects and that of the city's real estate industry improved when the recession receded.

Sadly, only a few months after closing that deal, a seemingly fit and healthy Sam Rudin—a natural athlete all his life, who jogged in Central Park into his late sixties and early seventies—suffered a fatal heart attack. He was not able to realize that everything he had planned and brought into existence in the real estate business had turned out fine.

Lew and Jack's mother May, who chaired the Samuel and May Rudin Foundation, lived until July 1992 and according to Lew, even flowered as the years went on. As the matriarch of the family's philanthropic arm in the wake of her husband's death, she helped oversee its disbursements, which were significant.[7] The numerous beneficiaries of the couple's largesse included medical charities and nursing scholarships to many different healthcare institutions, several AIDS-related programs, including the Incantation Children's Center (for infants), Columbia University's College of Physicians and Surgeons, and the Harlem Hospital Pediatrics Department, where the Rudin family foundation helped pioneer a hospital project that cares for sick infants outside often-crowded city hospitals and helps place them in foster homes. Other beneficiaries included Phoenix House, St. Luke's- Roosevelt Medical Center and Memorial Sloan-Kettering.

In the world of the arts and culture, the family's foundations supported Lincoln Center, the Metropolitan Museum of Art and the Museum of Natural History, to name just some of the cultural centers to benefit from May, as well as Lew and Jack Rudin's wealth. In education, the family's civic streak extended to supporting mentoring and after-school programs for public school students, as well as New York University,

Columbia University, Cooper Union, and Iona College. Most donations were made quietly and were virtually undetectable except of course to the institutions that received and put the money to work.

Lew revered his mother's singing and piano playing; she particularly enjoyed Irish ballads. She was also expert at crochet and needlepoint, loved novels, and read all the daily newspapers. Her culinary tastes ran to Chinese food and ice cream. Above all, May was no blushing rose. Lew recalled the day he brought her to the White House with his wife Rachel, his brother Jack, a then bushy-haired Bill, and Bill's daughter Samantha, who was not yet five years old. The occasion was an invitation to visit President George H. W. Bush in honor of May's ninety-second birthday. Lew Rudin noted in one interview that he and the president "used to kibitz about our mothers," and Lew staged a ballroom event for the president's "thousand points of light" message, encouraging people to volunteer on behalf of their neighbors and communities. His mother, who grew up as the daughter of the owner of a men's garment business on Long Island, looked elegant as she sat in the sunlit Oval Office that day, wearing a string of pearls and a floral dress. The visit lasted as much as a half-hour. When Lew's granddaughter whispered to her father that she'd like to see the Bush family dog Millie and her new puppies, the president said goodbye and the family was escorted out to the South Lawn.

"The least he could have done is have us for lunch," May said shortly afterward in a fancy Washington restaurant, Lew told an interviewer years later.[8] "She was just very strong and outspoken," he explained. "Though Americanized, she spoke Yiddish well. She had a quick, good sense of humor, and was very well read, reading all the time, right up until the end."

Her husband did not involve her very much in real estate, about which she was knowledgeable just the same. "She was a woman who was very concerned about her children, and making sure her husband didn't knock his brains out for others, as well as making sure her kids got what was due them. That was my mother," Lew added.

Whenever May Rudin sensed there had been a slight against any member of her immediate family, she did not quickly put it out of her mind. "If she didn't like anybody, that was it—there was no trying to convince her," Lew said.[9]

Like her husband, she had particular issues and causes that were important to her—nursing, for example, and education. She volunteered for the Red Cross during World War II and gave generously to nurse training programs. She took a keen interest in the Jewish Guild for the Blind and other organizations for the blind and disabled, such as the Lighthouse.

Growing up, Jack and Lew Rudin were raised by their parents in a Rudin Management building at 115 West Eighty-Sixth Street. They attended PS 166 on West Eighty-Ninth Street in a neighborhood that was largely Jewish and middle-class. The boys were very close and protective of each other while growing up, a time that featured games of street hockey on West Eighty-Seventh Street, playing basketball in Central Park, and gym activities and swimming at the local community center where they also studied on some afternoons. They ate pastrami on rye and sweet and sour pickles from the neighborhood's famous delis and frequented the West Side's movie houses. They especially delighted in ogling the life-size dinosaur skeletons and naturalistic dioramas in the Museum of Natural History, located practically in their backyard.

Jack was drafted into the Army in 1942 after graduating from DeWitt Clinton High School in the Bronx, which Lew, two years his junior, was still attending at the time. Lew would be drafted during his first year of college at NYU in 1945, and was trained as an infantry replacement for the planned Allied invasion of Japan. The anticipated tour of duty did not materialize, as President Harry Truman ordered the atomic bombs dropped on Hiroshima and Nagasaki, hastening the war's end. Instead, Lew was shipped overseas to Italy and there earned the rank of staff sergeant.

Jack's service proved more eventful than his younger brother's. He fought in Europe and saw combat in the Battle of the Bulge. He was awarded a Bronze Star and Combat Infantryman's Badge.

"Well, you know, I went from the summer of forty-two, wearing khaki in a Boy Scout camp, to three months later going into the Army," Jack said rather modestly many years later. "So at least the Army didn't have to teach me to mop a floor or make a bed or do KP."[10]

A photograph published in *Time* magazine in 1945, a "profile in courage," as it were, showed GIs crossing the Rhine River to invade Germany, one of them Jack Rudin. His shoulder patch identified him as a member of a famous American combat unit, the Rolling W (the Eighty-Ninth Infantry Division).

Jack was also among the soldiers who liberated Nazi concentration camps, where he witnessed prisoners' bodies stacked like cordwood, and the grateful albeit skeletal and horribly mistreated survivors. It was a scene he would always remember, and for him, and many other veterans, it gave meaning to his military sacrifice. It was perplexing, to say the least, when, in subsequent years, foreign leaders and even self-described historians sought for their own reasons or pathologies to deny that the Holocaust ever happened.

"It was a very strange feeling for anybody, especially someone who was Jewish, to see the camp. But we had no way of telling that the people we liberated were Jewish or otherwise," Jack recalled. "We assumed some were. There was no religious fervor in our efforts. We were trying to save all—whoever they were, men and women, regardless of religion."[11]

When Jack returned, his father brought him into the real estate business. He worked at construction sites to help learn the trade, while Lew went back to New York University to complete his bachelor's degree, majoring in real estate, and worked weekends in the family's renting office. Jack remained on the construction side and administrative side, while Lew worked on renting, financing, and marketing.

"Real estate was the family business," Lew said. "I grew up watching my father at work. In nineteen thirty-nine, he was building an apartment house at Two-Ninety-Five Central Park West and I saw him renting it. It was just written in the sand that I had to be in real estate."

The same was true for Jack. While the family thought it had built its last residential building in 1976, things changed when Rudin Management, under Bill and (Jack's son) Eric's leadership, began building new residential housing at a former medical center after the Greenwich Village hospital declared bankruptcy in 2008 and eventually closed its doors. The company, meanwhile, had continued erecting office buildings in the 1980s and '90s and into the 2000s, including the Reuters skyscraper at 3 Times Square, a three-year-long, thirty-two-story energy-efficient showcase project for the global media corporation, which was completed in 2001.

Like their father, the brothers prospered in the good times and persevered through the bad ones, seeking to stay-and-hold the portfolio ("Never sell!" Sam Rudin advised, describing his credo to fellow developers early in his career.)[12] The brothers mirrored their father's determination even in the wake of the devastating real estate crash of the early 1990s, when the family's net worth plummeted from $1.5 billion to $500 million and knocked them off the Forbes 400 list of the richest Americans.

During that real estate recession, the family's properties downtown suffered acutely when Drexel Burnham Lambert, the anchor tenant at the Rudin Management–owned 55 Broad Street, went bankrupt. The thirty-story office building on Broad was vacant for five years thereafter. Then, hours after reading a newspaper article reporting that Internet pioneer CompuServe was pondering a move to Manhattan, Lew, Jack, and Bill quickly decided to invest $40 million to turn the old, asbestos filled building into an Internet-ready "Information Technology Center," one of the first so-called smart buildings in the city. The conversion from a standard office building to a totally wired work environment made it attractive to technology firms. N2K, a digital music publisher, Sun Microsystems, and IBM were among those who moved to the address. The building was fully occupied in eighteen months.[13]

Within two weeks of the Rudins' decision to invest in the building's transformation and break new ground in the digital age for New York, then-mayor Rudy Giuliani embraced the project and its economic development potential for the Lower Manhattan business district, which had a glut of vacant office space. Along with the Rudins, the announcement to the assembled press in City Hall included members of the Downtown Alliance, a newly formed lower Manhattan business improvement district seeking a re-zoning to allow the ready conversion of languishing Wall Street–area office space for residential use. Prominent business leaders in finance and real estate were also on hand. While California had its Silicon Valley, the Rudins envisioned the start of a "Silicon Alley" for New York, and the city's commercial launch pad to the digital age.

Despite the Rudin family's success in real estate, Lew was in no way a cutthroat. Kenneth Langone, the venture capitalist, investment banker and financial backer and co-founder of The Home Depot, and one of New York City's leading philanthropists, recalled first meeting Lew Rudin in the 1970s shortly after the formation of ABNY. Langone was then in his mid-thirties and was the president of a medium-sized investment firm, R. W. Pressprich & Company. The firm had leased three floors in the Rudin building 80 Pine Street in the 1960s. By the early 1970s, the firm could not afford to keep all of the space. The chairman then suggested that Langone meet with Lew Rudin, whom he did not know and had never met even though Rudin was already a "legend in the city."[14] It was essential that Langone negotiate an agreement with Rudin Management to change the lease and occupy one-third of the space that they were then renting.[15]

Langone realized that Rudin could have played hardball and made it difficult for him and his firm. Langone was amazed that Lew's reaction was so positive. He allowed Pressprich to vacate two floors and remain with only one without asking for anything in return. Langone said that he "learned from Lew Rudin at this meeting that you do not have to beat the other guys in a deal to make a good deal, and you do not have to put your foot on the other guys to show how powerful you are.

"He was a wonderful man. I never had any reservation about doing business with the Rudins. They were elegant. The family has integrity, character, and whatever they did was ethical." Langone added, "My office is across the street from Bill Rudin's office. I did not want to get too far away from the Rudins."

3
Entree to Politics and Policy

Lew Rudin received one of his earliest lessons on the use of power in policymaking—and the importance of proximity to major officeholders—when he joined a group of landlords for a meeting with Governor Nelson Rockefeller in the late 1960s. As the availability of Manhattan office space tightened amid a shortage of new development, the city's commercial rents rose, and building owners feared a backlash to these inflationary pressures in the form of the imposition of commercial rent control by the state legislature. Lew himself was a staunch opponent of real estate price controls of all kinds, viewing them, as did his industry peers, as a barrier to new investment and development. Alton Marshall, Rockefeller's chief of staff, remembered a "kind of skinny, fuzzy haired young man"—Rudin—sitting there among a group of visiting real estate "graybeards." The governor was late to the meeting and when he finally arrived, he stayed only long enough to get the gist of why the real estate men had come.

"I have to go," the peripatetic Rockefeller said, "but Al here will be here, and whatever Al says, goes."

"The governor then walked out," Marshall recalled in 2002.[1]

"I had heard all I wanted to hear, and I said to this group, 'There won't be any commercial rent control.'" That was that. Rudin never got over it, Marshall said, referring to the notion that someone could just sit there and speak with so much confidence and certainty about what stood at the time as the real estate men's topmost concern—and was clearly a concern to Rudin Management as well, given its own stake in commercial properties and office tenants—not to mention a contentious public issue.

To Rudin, then a political neophyte, this was a lesson in how policy was shaped and executed, at times by a wave of a powerful governor's hand or that of his chief of staff. You could have great ideas, but ultimately it was personal contact with those in power that seemed to matter a great deal or even the most.

The meeting was also Marshall's first introduction to Rudin.

"My first impression was of a young man of considerable sincerity, probably not terribly sophisticated, but certainly bound up with all the energy and conviction of his ideas about what we should be doing about helping New York City," he said.[2]

Though the industry received personal assurances from Alton Marshall that commercial rent control was not going to become a reality, the developers responded to the groundswell for commercial rent increase limitations by putting together an informal arbitration panel before which business owners facing steep increases could appeal to a group of owners for a reduced hike.

In this way, it was hoped, the most disgruntled tenants would resist the temptation to join with those pushing in Albany for the kind of rent controls that had existed for residential leases since World War II. It was also hoped they would resist joining the departure of large companies attracted to the tax breaks and lower rents offered by the New York suburbs and the South and the Southwest, where growth was more and more being subsidized by the federal government with the same level of generosity once enjoyed by older port cities such as New York.

The companies threatening to leave or actually doing so in the 1950s and 1960s were often apt to cite a litany of complaints about the declining condition of the city, including aging subways, crime, and increasingly troubled schools in some areas, as well as the cost of taxes and electricity. For them, it was not just about rents. Would the voices of corporate dissatisfaction prompt an increase in corporate departures?, Rudin and fellow real estate owners asked. Would demand for their offices and apartments drop? Would New York City go the way of fading industrial cities like Detroit?

Rudin was eager to participate in the solution, and did. It was the beginning of his civic involvement. Interestingly, in all his subsequent attempts to assist elected leaders, he was rarely seen as a landlord motivated by self-enrichment. Though he never denied wanting his civic prominence to have a salutary and profitable effect on the value of his family real estate holdings, he was careful to avoid giving anyone a legitimate reason to suspect that he sought or received a quid pro quo for all his civic-minded work. "The secret of my relationship with the political world is I never ask them for anything," he once said, according to the *New York Times.* "So I owe them nothing. Most of the time, they owe *me* something."[3]

In the early 1970s, Lew and Jack even turned down a once-in-a-lifetime invitation from Michael Burke, president of the New York Yankees, which was owned by CBS at the time. CBS was looking to sell part or all of the team to a mix of investors.

Lew decided, according to his son, Bill, that he didn't want his public support of the city's controversial renovation of Yankee Stadium in the 1970s to be perceived as having been motivated by any desire to become a future co-owner of New York's most storied sports franchise. The Rudin brothers demurred. Years later, Jack Rudin expressed relief: "We missed the biggest excitement of our life, thank God. . . . We'd have spent all our time uptown, shagging flies."[4]

"Lew never, ever, was promoting his own real estate while he was promoting New York," said Howard Rubenstein, "That was his bible: 'I'm promoting New York, not my own buildings.' And that helped ABNY become successful."[5]

Something that Lew could not ignore were the grim headlines and newscasts of the 1960s and '70s about the rising instances of shootings of police officers. He was especially troubled that New York City police officers, unlike many of their counterparts elsewhere, lacked a proven form of protection—bulletproof vests—that could save them from becoming casualties of increasing handgun violence. When the Patrolmen's Benevolent Association president Sam DeMilia called him one day and complained that city leaders, emphasizing the city's budgetary constraints, were refusing to set aside funds to purchase the protection, Rudin jumped in and helped the New York City Police Foundation—then a fledgling nonprofit organization, created to further the priorities of the city police commissioner—raise private money to help the city make the purchases. Lew Rudin's daughter Beth recalled that her father was "horrified" to hear that the city was leaving police officers exposed, especially since the vests cost about $1,500 apiece, a small price to pay, he felt, to protect officers from injury or death.[6]

It might have been a no-brainer to Rudin, but at the time, in the late 1970s, some security experts questioned the effectiveness of the vests, and some police officers considered the protection too bulky and uncomfortable to be worth the trouble to wear throughout their shifts. In addition, it was a time of severe austerity, so city funding was difficult if not impossible to come by, even for worthy initiatives.

Making matters more difficult, the ensuing negotiations between the Police Foundation, whose executive director was Betsy Gotbaum, and the PBA's DeMilia did not go smoothly, recalled Gotbaum. Pamela Delaney, who was an assistant in the city police commissioner's office and the Police Department's liaison to the Police Foundation, remembers that the union did not trust the management-linked Foundation to represent its interests fully, though Gotbaum was the wife of Victor Gotbaum, leader of the largest municipal union of the city.[7] Disagreements flared over the bid price for the vests, but both sides, with Rudin's close involvement, finally accepted a competitive rate offered by a Pennsylvania manufacturing firm with a union workforce.[8]

Under the vest-purchasing program, the money for the purchase was raised from major business institutions such as Citibank and of course Rudin's own resources, a contribution that Mary Holloway, who became ABNY's executive director in 1979, estimated to be approximately $1 million.[9] Powerful Brooklyn (Kings County) Democratic leader Meade Esposito and Louis Nizer, a noted and distinguished trial lawyer, worked with Rudin and the Foundation on the campaign.

Throughout the often testy negotiations, Rudin counseled care and diplomacy and no public finger pointing, said Betsy Gotbaum. At the same time, according to the recollections of Delaney, who was the NYPD's liaison to the Foundation, Rudin privately complained about the months of delays. "'C'mon,' he'd say. 'Let's cut through all this bullshit, this is a perfect role for the Police Foundation and the Association for a Better New York to play, and we can join hands with the union that is really pushing this, and raise the private funds to do this,'" recalled Delaney.

As a builder very familiar with the cost of red tape and delay, Rudin did not suffer bureaucratic encumbrances or foot dragging gladly, though they could not have surprised him in a city with so many clashing super-egos and mega-interests and a long and well-publicized historical record of corruption and scandal across local and state government and the private sector alike. With the help of his unremitting kibitzing and phone calls, however, mutual suspicions among the different parties were suspended. Nearly $1.5 million was cobbled together from private contributions in all, covering the initial buy of 1,500 vests under a city-approved pilot project funded through the Police Foundation.

Within three years, virtually every police officer in the city had the protective gear. Mayor Ed Koch would add bulletproof vests to the standard equipment issued to tens of thousands of transit and housing police officers as well, while subsequent fundraising campaigns in which Rudin also participated helped the city replace the initial vests with newer technology.

It was never a panacea—Koch would attend thirty-nine police funerals in his twelve years in office, a reflection of the city's relentless gun violence.[10] However, it did save lives, and that was what Rudin hoped it would do. In addition, the effort showed that the city government, even when pinched for revenue, could respond to a genuine need in partnership with the private sector and the municipal unions. In subsequent years, public-private partnerships would become more common, with funds from private donors and nonprofit organizations improving lackluster neighborhood streets and bedraggled parks throughout the five boroughs. These partnerships have included Business Improvement Districts (BIDs), which direct fees or supplemental tax assessments to projects and programs within the districts, as well as parks foundations such as the Central Park Conservancy, the Prospect Park Alliance, and Friends of the High Line that both raise funds and provide management for existing and new city parks.

Years after his father helped spearhead the vest buying campaign, Bill Rudin was surprised and gratified when the son of a New York City police officer approached him and thanked him. The younger man, who was now a police officer himself, said that the bulletproof vests that Lew had helped fund had saved the lives of many police officers including friends of his own father. Bill, for his part, said he felt gratified and proud.[11]

Especially with the help of hindsight, Rudin's civic contribution can be seen to have had an enduring impact, strengthening the city's foundation, which was often his ultimate goal. His enlightened self-interest could not be said to be common. It set him apart from CEOs and many other real estate developers who did not see any compelling reason to take time away from their companies to devote to the general welfare of the city in which they worked and sometimes resided.

"You find very few people in the private world who would cross the line and say, 'I want to help the government,'" Jack Nyman, dean of the Steven L. Newman Real Estate Institute at Baruch College," told *The Real Deal,* a publication that covers the New York real estate business, in 2008. "But Lew knew that for his residential holdings and for his office buildings, he had to keep the city going."[12]

So it was that although Lew's father, Sam, advised him to steer clear of the city's very serious fiscal problems in the 1970s, Lew Rudin, to no one's surprise, disagreed with his well-meaning, business-focused dad.

"But Pop," Lew said, "it *is* my business."

Rudin described his views in a radio interview with John Wingate of WOR-AM in 1974, when the city still had a major housing crisis, crumbling infrastructure, and swelling welfare rolls, and many schools were overcrowded, antiquated, and failing. Crime, too, was on the way to becoming the top issue of the 1977 mayoral race in which Ed Koch, a new convert to the death penalty, would beat out a field of seven Democratic contenders, including Mario Cuomo and the incumbent, Abe Beame.

"I live in the city" Rudin said, "and I went to public school and public high school, DeWitt Clinton. And except for an occasional trip—I used to be a summer resident in Long Beach, Long Island; except for that and being in the Army, I lived in the city, and still live in the city, and hope to live here the rest of my life. My children have been brought up in the city, except for college. I went to New York University. So I—you know, I'm a born and bred lover of the city."[13]

So it was personal as well as business—his personality and inventory were anchored solidly and permanently in the granite floor of the city.

"We had to do something," Rudin would say years later, looking back at the 1970s recession and other economic downspin he lived through. "We couldn't very well pick up our buildings and move them across the George Washington Bridge!"

Felix Rohatyn, the Wall Street financier who during the 1975 fiscal crisis year served as a critical bridge to the financial industry and a key advisor for Governor Hugh Carey, said, "Even though everybody knew that Lew and his family had enormous real estate interests in this city, it was always clear that the only thing that really interested him was the city. Lew was the ultimate New Yorker. He cared for the city about as passionately as anybody that I saw then or now."[14]

The late Percy Sutton, who was Manhattan borough president from 1966 to 1977 (when he ran for mayor), agreed. "Other people in politics, such as the governor, all rose to meet the 1975 fiscal crisis, but if Lew had not stood up and said 'Let's organize to save this city,' I'm not sure how we would have come out at that particular juncture. He gave the impetus that was necessary in a city so dependent upon real estate taxes and upon the quality of the people who run the giant real estate firms," Sutton said.[15]

The sentiment was also echoed by Alton Marshall, former governor Nelson Rockefeller's chief of staff who was later the president of Rockefeller Center. Rudin, he said, "was indeed Mister New York. I mean, the unofficial mayor."[16]

It is interesting to recall that a former New York City police commissioner—Grover Whalen—had also been known widely as "Mr. New York." Whalen, who served in a series of administrative positions in several mayoral administrations in the early to mid-twentieth century, was perhaps best known as the city's honorary greeter and booster, beginning during Fiorello LaGuardia's three eventful terms as mayor. Until the early 1950s, Whalen, who titled his memoir *Mr. New York*, opened doors for visiting VIP's as they arrived in limousines at City Hall, or strode to the end of the tarmac at LaGuardia Airport to welcome a monarch, general, or prime minister descending from a plane. He marched in many ticker tape parades for world figures and was credited with making the confetti-strewn Wall Street canyon spectacle a New York City staple. He was a bearish and recognizable figure in a Homburg hat, with a white chrysanthemum pinned to his pinstriped suit.[17]

While Rudin, in a much modernized New York City era, enjoyed handing out tiny golden apple ornaments, his version of "Mr. New York" and chief booster of all things New York was decidedly different. Though he never ran for political office or held a major appointive position in government, his contributions were substantive and numerous. The imprint he and his business partner brother Jack made was tangible and extensive.

Rudin touched off the creation of a new city agency that helped a dwindling film and television industry grow into a thriving segment of the local economy and a potent advertisement and tourism engine for New York.[18] Lew rallied businessmen and politicians to revive the ailing Lincoln Center Theater—of which he was a founding board member when the theater was established in 1984—at a point when it fell upon hard times and confronted near-insolvency, helping to rescue a vital component of the cultural and artistic landscape. He was a founding member of the theater's board. Jack, meanwhile, played a significant role in creating Jazz at Lincoln Center in the 1990s.

The Rudin brothers also helped reinvent and popularize the New York City Marathon, sparking its transformation from a humble Central Park race into a citywide competition of worldwide renown. Lew was critical to seeing through the city's efforts in the 1970s and again in the '90s to keep the United States Tennis Association in New York, with the complete support of mayors Abe Beame, Ed Koch, and the tennis-loving David Dinkins.[19]

Lew helped lead a national push by New York and other large states in the 1980s that ultimately prevented the elimination of the tax deduction for state and local taxes on federal tax returns during the overhaul of the tax code.[20] Rudin went to Washington and, backed by many of the city's business elites, defeated it.

He was not only a cheerleader, then, shouting encouragement from the sidelines. He brought about and catalyzed change.

He did not conform easily to the pat characterizations by those who viewed the city's landlords like him as self-serving, permanent power brokers.

Even though he was included by Jack Newfield and Paul Du Brul as one of the city's unelected power brokers in their 1977 work *The Abuse of Power: The Permanent Government and the Fall of New York,* Rudin, despite his wealth and connections, hardly resembled the composite sketch the authors painted of the clubhouse boss or greedy business chieftain bent on manipulating city government for his own benefit. The Rudin brothers argued for revival of languishing federal tax credits to support the construction and maintenance of low-income and middle-class housing and worked with and supported the aims of civil service unions for retirement security and a living wage. They were also in support of federal legislation to liberalize the U.S. immigration policies, keenly appreciative of the regenerative power of immigration for faded city neighborhoods and aware of and sympathetic to the difficulties faced by newcomers and the poor. No one needed to convince the Rudin brothers of the importance and value of a sturdy and broad safety net for the disadvantaged, the sick, and the elderly.

Aware of the great wealth and advantages in which he was born, Rudin remained on the lookout throughout his adult life for ways to share his family's wealth with those whom it might benefit, the better to allow the beneficiary organizations to work in concert for more societal improvements. He served as a trustee at Carnegie Hall, Meals on Wheels, New York University, the Lincoln Center Theater, Lenox Hill Hospital, the Citizens Crime Commission, the New York City Police Foundation, the New York City Partnership, the Federation of Jewish Philanthropies of New York, Mentoring USA (which focused on curbing the dropout rate), and The Help (an organization to assist the homeless).

While he viewed philanthropy and commerce as important levers of civic improvement in the city, Rudin by no means saw the private sector as the only tool in the box. Instead, he strongly believed in working with every sector.

Victor Gotbaum, who for decades led District Council 37 of the American Federation of State, County and Municipal Employees, the largest union for city workers, stated that, "I guess the fiscal crisis of nineteen seventy-five was the first time I met Lew. But even before then, like everybody else I 'exploited' Lew"—and the union leader laughed. "If you needed something, you went to Lew. [Years later, after leaving DC 37], I was teaching at the CUNY Graduate School and I had a lot of poor students. Lew was one of the guys I would go to, and say: Lew, I need this, that. He'd never turn you down. You know he'd give you money for these kids, which was really nice."[21]

It was a common refrain. Once, in 1979, when Dr. O. Wayne Isom, a physician Rudin saw regularly, mentioned the devastation a hurricane had brought to the 100,000-person city of Wichita Falls, Texas (Isom's home state), Rudin and a few other New York businessmen recruited by him raised several hundred thousand dollars and sent the check to the beleaguered city's mayor. The mayor eventually repaid Rudin with the Key to the City and made him an honorary citizen.

Isom, a cardiothoracic specialist, had never asked his patient to help Wichita Falls, but Lew took it upon himself to do so, and Isom always suspected that most if not all of the money came from him. "As I got to know Lew, and I saw all the things that he did for New York City, for all ethnic groups, all religions, every group of people in New York, it made me feel he was not just an altruistic New Yorker, but just an altruistic American. He cared about everybody,"[22] the physician said.

When in the early 1980s Lew's daughter Beth explained the difficulties the Gay Men's Health Crisis was experiencing in raising money (one of the grassroots group's founders, Nathan Kolodner, was Beth's good friend), the family foundation gave the group a $25,000 grant, which was one of the largest private donations to GMHC at the time. The donation to the fledgling organization conveyed an imprimatur, thus giving GMHC entree to many other foundations from which it could gain needed financial support in a period of national paranoia and loathing about AIDS and amidst many campaigns to stigmatize its adult and child victims.[23]

Lew stood ready to involve himself in the issues and problems he felt were important, his daughter said years later. This stance, or readiness, can provide inspiration to a new generation of urban and national organizations grappling with the effects of growing disparities in wealth, health, and education in America, environmental risks such as global warming, and many other local and international concerns.

Rudin understood that public questions that were facing New York, other large cities, and the country as a whole could never be solved in any serious way by government actions alone. He sought to coax the private sector to participate and partner with the public sector, and he forged seminal public-private partnerships at a time when the concept was relatively untested and even unnamed. His goal was to help the government, however imperfect, to do its work and the city and its real estate community to confront looming threats to its prosperity and development.

"My father loved New York and wanted to reward New York for what it did for our family," noted Bill Rudin, who became president of Rudin Management in 1993, more than a half-century after its incorporation. "It was as simple as that."[24]

4
Birth of the Association for a Better New York

The talk was all about the condition of the city and what to do about it when the Association for a Better New York, or ABNY, first took shape in the early months of 1971. Rudin, then forty-four, wearing his familiar vintage pilot's glasses, sat down for breakfast at the Regency Hotel on Park Avenue one cold January morning, together with a small gathering of fellow businessmen and friends. Writing on the back of an envelope, they framed out an organization that would grow to encompass 125 business leaders. Initially, the group had a budget for three years, with $2.5 million donated from its members, the fees varying and based on each company's square footage in Manhattan. The group set out to operate much as a chamber of commerce does in smaller cities, boosting the city's image and pressing for improvements for the sake of tourism and the business climate. (The New York Chamber of Commerce, founded in 1768 by a group of city merchants, and the first commercial organization of its kind, was relatively dormant.)

There were notable precursors. One business-led group grew out of an effort in the early 1960s led by Clarence Francis, then the retired chairman of General Foods. His company had turned heads in 1951 when it announced that its corporate headquarters was leaving Park Avenue for a more garden-like campus with ample parking in Westchester County's White Plains, taking 1,300 administrative jobs with it. In 1965, after many other businesses followed General Foods out of the city, Francis helped start the Economic Development Council of New York City (EDC), a private group made up of twenty-six leading corporate executives, as a response to what he and other business leaders felt was the city government's chronic inattention to business development and retention. The group sponsored executives-on-loan efforts and other business support programs while backing the Lindsay administration's state legislative agenda, including its successful push for the introduction of a fractional income tax on commuters from outside the city to help pay for municipal services (though the commuter tax, which brought the city $500 million annually, would be eliminated in the late 1990s during a fierce partisan political battle in Albany).[1] Through the EDC, the CEOs of some Fortune 500 companies formed a communication bridge to City Hall, and the Lindsay administration eventually launched the first city Economic Development Administration—or EDA—to locate at City Hall all public sector–led efforts to attract and retain corporations with tax breaks and other assistance.[2]

Eight years after ABNY's founding, David Rockefeller of Chase Manhattan Bank co-founded the New York City Partnership, a blue-chip coalition of chief executive officers in finance, insurance, and real estate, which promoted a developmental agenda and business growth for the city. After merging with the New York Chamber of Commerce in 2002, it continues to do so to this day as the Partnership for New York City.

But in 1971, it was the New York real estate leaders, those who were closer to the business mood of Main Street than were the heads of Fortune 500 companies, who began tackling the complaints they were hearing from their tenants about the corroding business and social climate in many parts of Manhattan.

As scrappy as he could be, Lew was a somewhat unlikely figure to lead a new business coalition of this sort. He was not a figure of influence from a major corporation, or even a highly recognizable leader yet of his industry. His prominent and respected father was still alive, and his brother Jack was two years older than Lew. "He was a young guy with big glasses," remembered Jay Kriegel, who was then the chief of staff to Mayor John Lindsay.[3] Still, he added, Mayor Lindsay and city department heads appreciated Rudin's and ABNY's willingness to help City Hall and department heads with their various initiatives.

These were years when the city was roiled by labor strikes, and even Mayor Lindsay was met on his very first day in office by a citywide subway strike. There existed a deep-seated and spreading poverty, growing racial tensions, and headline-grabbing scandals in corporate executive suites and the police department and other agencies. Social, economic, and political tumult stemming from the Vietnam War, the military draft, and baby boomers' distrust of authority figures stirred many conflicts that played out on the city's streets, in its parks, public schools, universities, and government chambers.

In Rudin's vision, ABNY would not aim to cover any single geographical area of the city, as did another David Rockefeller–led group, the Downtown-Lower Manhattan Association. He also did not want his group to become bogged down researching and proposing broad new public policies, the domain of the business-supported Citizens Budget

Commission and the venerable Regional Planning Association. Rudin also did not want ABNY to lobby for the real estate industry, as the Real Estate Board of New York, of which the Rudin brothers were members, already did so.

Nor did Rudin envision ABNY's focusing on real estate issues per se, like the Associated Builders and Owners of Greater New York, a meaningful political voice under the developer and liberal social activist Maurice Paprin in the 1970s and '80s for residential builders and investor owners. (This group pressed for a reduction in rent regulations and for increases in state and federal subsidies and tax abatements for the construction of low- and moderately-priced new housing in New York, of which there was a shortage.)

Instead of doing all of those things, ABNY set out chiefly to defend the city's much-maligned image, playing up its well-known merits, and seeking to prod and assist local government officials to address issues of quality of life, particularly those affecting property values, commerce, and tourism.

Although ABNY's membership rolls spanned many types of businesses, ABNY's core activists were, in fact, big developers, "guys who were entrepreneurial. They owned their own businesses. They didn't consult boards of directors. They weren't surrounded by government relations people and lawyers," said Jay Kriegel, who would join the ABNY executive board after serving in the Lindsay administration. He described their hands-on involvement and orientation as a plus for the new organization.

Just as significantly, the fate of the members' businesses and bottom lines were closely interdependent with the state of the New York economy, making the landlords especially sensitive to signs of broad economic weaknesses, and sensitive to the urgency for prompt remedies. "The real estate guys have nowhere else to go; this is their home. This is their sole interest," explained Kriegel.[4]

In the 1950s, the total number of Fortune 500 corporations with their headquarters in the city's central business district and the Wall Street area was 140. By the mid-1970s, the figure was down to 84.[5] There were still a total of 450 national companies of all types in the midtown central business district by the mid-1980s, principally financial institutions and large producer- and business-service firms of the type that allowed New York to promote itself as a global city.[6] ABNY, however, shook the red flag of warning most vigorously and earlier than most, as it saw middle-class residents leaving en masse for the booming suburbs, and many businesses—their commercial tenants—going too, drawn by lower labor, land, tax and energy costs, and, of course, fewer worries about their employees becoming the victims of pickpockets or muggers.

"We were losing some tenants, yes," Rudin said years later, recalling his decision to start ABNY. "It was self-interest on our part, obviously, but we knew that to save the city and to save ourselves, we had to improve the environment around our buildings."[7] The city's 1975 fiscal crisis, which would catch nearly everyone, including ABNY, by surprise, was still more than four years away when the group began, but the complex mixture of problems that helped give rise to that watershed crisis year were already stirring, and symptoms of the city's budgetary distress could be detected in neglect of parks, abandonment of old buildings, rubble-strewn and barren lots, and the spreading litter and graffiti.

"We're all tired of forming groups and committees, but we had to do something, and this is really a desperation move," commented Preston Robert Tisch, then president of the Loews hotel and theater enterprises and head of the New York City Convention and Visitors Bureau, to the *New York Times*. The article on the group by the paper of record described its formation and its release of a pro–New York City brochure.[8]

Tisch told the newspaper that he was attracted to the idea of forming the association after the General Telephone and Electronics Corporation had announced it was moving its headquarters from Manhattan to Connecticut, for him and many others a distressing turn of events. In addition to Rudin and Tisch, the founding ABNY executive committee included Rexford Tompkins, a banker who in 1972 became president of the Real Estate Board of New York; Alton Marshall, who was president of Rockefeller Center after having worked for Governor Rockefeller; Alan V. Tishman of Tishman Realty; Irving Schneider, executive vice president of Helmsley-Spear Inc.; and real estate developer Charles Benenson. Howard Rubenstein, the public relations strategist, was also key to the founding and future development of the association. Rubenstein's growing connections and clients would one day rival those of Rudin, and the two men worked closely from ABNY's conception to develop its reach and impact for many years.[9]

The new entity was no fly-by-night group. It extended outward from real estate owners to include 127 members representing mercantile and banking interests, and was formed, the *Times* article dutifully noted, after consultation with Mayor Lindsay and Governor Rockefeller. The earliest action agenda of the organization included plans for a street-cleaning program in the midtown area. The group said it would seek to create shuttle service between Grand Central and Pennsylvania

Station, and promote construction of a city convention center near the Hudson River. Its members called for special programs to help improve the schools and the eligibility of their graduates to go directly into business.

Rexford Tompkins said the creation of ABNY's first brochure, which touted the business advantages, did not suggest that the group only intended to perform cheerleading. "If we're just going to be a booster club," he said, "who needs it? What we're trying to do is get a business presence involved with New York problems. Then existing organizations can go forward."[10]

"I think an attitude is developing in the business community—they're willing to accept responsibility," Alton Marshall said at the time. "They realize that it's their problem, not just Lindsay's or the governor's. After all, there's no better motivation than a selfish one."[11]

In the ensuing years, as the city's problems deepened and its reputation worsened, Rudin made numerous radio and television appearances to explain the association's mission. ABNY would enlarge its initial budget and make itself known in the debates to come about how best to reverse declining physical and social conditions in and around the business sections of Manhattan.

"I think what we're really aiming to do is to convince many of the middle-income and corporate leaders of the city to stay in the city and not to move their businesses and homes to the Connecticut area or to Westchester or Jersey or St. Louis or Houston," Lew said on a Channel 9 Sunday morning news program in September 1972. "I think this is the place they'll find they can do the best business, they can find that they've got the greatest theater, the greatest restaurants, the greatest schools—we're a college town, don't let anybody mistake it. And I think you're going to hear more and more of that."[12]

With Tisch, Schneider, and Rubenstein and others connected to real estate and tourism, and with Bill Swan's help as ABNY executive director, Rudin and ABNY soon after its formation launched Operation Clean Sweep, which encouraged building owners to have their own janitorial staffs sweep the sidewalks, gutters, and streets of debris each day. The operation could have been perceived as an incursion on municipal labor's turf, but Rudin enlisted the support of, and became friends with, the labor leader John DeLury of the sanitation workers union, someone to whom he was introduced by the union's representative, Jack Bigel.

DeLury, an old-time labor leader and native New Yorker, handed Rudin and his friends big brooms and shovels on the first day, to go along with their blue blazers and shiny shoes. He then walked them into the streets around Grand Central Terminal—where they went to work with gusto. "These guys, who probably hadn't dirtied their hands except when playing golf, really started cleaning the streets around Grand Central," said Bigel, interviewed years later. It was largely a photo opportunity, cooked up by public relations expert Rubenstein, and supportive of Mayor Lindsay's "Don't Be a Litter Bug" advertising campaign. But in truth, as Bigel detected, it was also part of something more.[13]

"They had both exercise and pictures," said Bigel. "The pictures were printed in the newspapers and the exercise undoubtedly added to their good health. Then we brought Lewis into the sanitation garages at five in the morning so he could meet two hundred or so drivers, loaders, before they took the trucks out. This went on for a couple of weeks and had a great effect on the morale of those workers, and Lewis was able to see what people do to help run the city."

Initially, according to Bigel, DeLury viewed the wealthy real estate developers and other business honchos warily, "but when he saw Lewis with a broom in his hand, and visiting garages, I'd say that turned over completely, and he accepted Lewis, and not only accepted him, but he would greet him very warmly. This really continued right up through the thirty-odd years that Lewis spearheaded ABNY."

Above all, Rudin's success with ABNY lay in the fact that he was, to most people he encountered, sincere in his desire to help, and likeable, Matilda Cuomo, wife of the three-term Democratic New York State governor Mario Cuomo, and mother of the current governor, Andrew Cuomo, once observed. Mrs. Cuomo said, "Some people put on airs. Some people are condescending in their positions in life. But not Lew. Lew could be with a queen, with a king, it didn't matter—it was always Lew. Lew was himself. And that is a remarkable trait, it really is."[14]

In its first year, ABNY also raised funds for another significant public initiative, one enlisting doormen to fight petty crime and outfitting them with walkie-talkies, code numbers, and training to help them watch streets, corridors, and other byways and report to the police any indication of anything threatening. Rubenstein came up with the name: "Operation Interlock."

George Lence was among a dedicated cadre of Forest Hills High School students who worked as summer interns at ABNY. One day, the teenagers were dispatched by Rudin and Tisch into midtown streets to snap Polaroid photos of storefronts. They followed up with a typed letter signed by

Lew Rudin. One version of the letter praised merchants for their tidiness, while the other called on other, less-than-tidy storekeepers to improve the appearance of their shops.

"I have great memories of working that summer at ABNY because it really was a tough time for the city, and we were literally going door-to-door to improve it," said Lence, now an attorney and the president of a New York communications consulting firm.[15]

ABNY early on also worked assiduously with city agencies to try to stem the proliferation of porn parlors and peep shows in Times Square and to increase police presence and lighting in the Broadway theater district. It launched a program designed to make the public aware that by placing their Social Security number on personal objects of value and registering the number with their local police precinct, the items would be more traceable if stolen, and might even deter theft in the first place.

In addition, there was "Adopt a Park," which encouraged businesses to work to improve their local parks, and "PACT"—Provide Addict Care Today—to ensure that recovering heroin addicts received access to methadone treatment. Fresh ideas came pouring out of ABNY. "Daylight Savings Time" publicized the need for year-round daylight savings time to delay the onset of darkness, when most crimes occurred. "Labor Relations" was a program that set up a dialogue between the city's uniformed and municipal unions. Manhattan parks, frequented each lunch hour by city office workers, were brightened by ABNY personnel with spring plantings.

It all added up to something positive. The ideas, idealism, and sweat equity sponsored by ABNY and other business and community groups could not alone overcome the profound problems facing the city during this brutal recession and population decline. However, the partnership of ABNY with state and local government continued and was of aid in getting out of the fiscal crisis. As Felix Rohaytn said in an interview, "We were operating on different but parallel levels, and working towards a common goal."[16]

5
The Film and Television Industry Comes of Age in New York City

In 1974, a thriller set in New York was headed toward final production, and needed the approval of city officials so filming could take place in the city's subway system and other locations around town. The film, however, was not exactly a positive portrayal of life in New York City. It focused on four heavily armed criminals with code names "Mr. Blue, Mr. Green, Mr. Grey, and Mr. Brown." According to the script, they hijack a crowded subway car and hold the trapped and frightened straphangers for $1 million ransom from the city.

Leaders in the movie industry and some New York officials who read the script of *The Taking of Pelham One Two Three* felt it captured the nagging sense many had that the city was no longer the master of its own destiny. It even included a fictional mayor who agrees to the hijackers' ransom demand when their leader, wearing a disguise and speaking in a British accent, threatens to kill the passengers one by one on the runaway train if the money is not delivered.

What was not known when the film was planned for production was that Mayor Abe Beame had serious reservations about the movie. In fact, he attempted to discourage and prevent *The Taking of Pelham One Two Three* after reading the script, provided by people associated with the project seeking the city's cooperation.

Hearing about the mayor's resistance to the project, Gabriel Katzka, a producer involved in the project, phoned Lew Rudin to see if he would speak with Beame about it. Rudin agreed and then got in touch with a neighbor who was one of the few people he knew in the entertainment business—the talent manager and producer Martin Bregman.

The New York City–born Bregman, who during his career managed and brought to public attention such stars as Woody Allen, Barbra Streisand, Liza Minnelli, and Bette Midler, had already produced or co-produced two outstanding crime films set and filmed in the city, *Dog Day Afternoon* (1975) and *Serpico* (1973). He would help to produce at least thirty-three other films in the years to follow. While he, like Rudin, had no connection to the subway hijacking film project, and knew Katzka only slightly, he agreed to accompany Rudin to City Hall because as a matter of principle he did not like the idea of any elected official's interfering with a creative project of any kind. On top of that, he knew Rudin socially, and found him to be "a very real person; there are not that many real people in this world, or so you find out as you get older—people who care." So he went along to see the mayor.

The private meeting of Bregman, Rudin, and Beame didn't go smoothly. Bregman remembered that he expressed the view that elected officials had no business getting in the way of a writer's script or a film's direction, as that would amount to censorship. The mayor, however, did not budge, reiterating that he did not want to see a negative script with a scary New York City scenario turned into a realistic feature film, according to Bregman.

As the standoff grew, voices were raised and, Bregman recalled, he and Beame began yelling at each other.

Bregman at the same time knew he had no real political power, and would not have had an audience with the powerful Democrat were it not for Rudin, a friend of Beame. Rudin was "my muscle," he recalled, and since the moviemaker's muscle was sitting right next to him, nodding in agreement, Beame must have felt compelled to sit an hour or so and participate actively in the debate, rather than go back to his work.

After a while, Rudin spoke up, offering a suggestion that struck Bregman as thoughtful: Why not take the reverse position, Mr. Mayor, and create a film office to assist in the development of the film and television production industry in the city? Rudin assured Beame that he would get a great deal of credit if movie and television production increased and brought jobs to New York smack in the middle of a bad recession.

With that, Beame "just backed off," said Bregman, who took the lead in helping put together the new city office. Bregman moved quickly thereafter, putting film industry professionals in charge of it and organizing the cooperation and participation of Actor's Equity, the Teamsters, and other unions involved in the industry. *The Taking of Pelham One Two Three* finally got going, and within months the newly created New York City Office of Film and Television Production became the first office of its kind nationally. The new office set itself to simplifying the work of film and television productions in getting streets temporarily closed, gaining police protection for moveable sidewalk sets, winning city permits, and limiting working with neighborhoods during shoots. The office also worked to provide tax credits to help make the city known as an attractive place in which to film motion pictures and television shows.

While filmmaking and television production were an estimated $400,000-a-year industry in the city at the time of Rudin's inspired suggestion to create a new office dedicated to its cultivation, it grew within two years into a $4 million business. Today, it is common to bump into a film or television show production filming on city streets, while several new studios have opened around the city. Dozens of television shows and motion pictures are made in the city each year. Among the productions have been *Sex and the City*, the *Law & Order* series, *The Daily Show*, and *The Amazing Spider-Man*. With the help of what is now known as the Mayor's Office of Film, Theatre & Broadcasting, along with state and city tax incentives, the entertainment industry in the city generates billions of dollars in business and jobs, according to *Business Week*.[1]

Characteristically, Lew Rudin never took credit for helping to create the film and television office, nor did he benefit from it in any way personally, said Bregman. "But Lew was responsible for it. Without him, it wouldn't have happened. I believe that we would not now have a flourishing film and television industry here. And we're a big industry, a huge industry."[2]

6
The Looming New York City Fiscal Crisis

By 1974, few, including Lew Rudin and his Association for a Better New York, could possibly have appreciated or known that the worst economic disaster to hit the New York City government since the Great Depression was lurking like a mugger just around the corner. But Rudin would be among the first people to rush to the city's rescue, and keep it from defaulting on its payment obligations, once the signs of distress became plainly visible.

At first, the only eyebrows that were raised about the city government's tenuous financial condition arched subtly under bankers' figurative green eyeshades in private City Hall meetings between Beame administration officials and representatives of the banks. The representatives quietly but persistently told the then–newly elected mayor Abe Beame and City Comptroller Harrison J. Goldin about their growing difficulties attracting institutional and individual investors for the city's bonds and notes. The bankers soon indicated that they would have to raise the interest rates the city offered the investment community in order to ensure that the municipal debt paper remained marketable and in demand, even with its triple-tax deductibility on state, city, and federal taxes. The city's bonds, whose underwriting and sale were handled by banks that competed for the profitable business—and that bought them themselves—were necessary to generate from investors the long-range capital financing needed to build and repair hospitals, schools, highways, bridges. Adding to the city's need for the loans, its capital spending was not keeping up with the city's aging infrastructure at the time. A portion of the West Side Highway collapsed in 1973, a crashing symbol of the city's much-deferred repair needs.

The negative talk among bankers in 1974 and into 1975 upset and angered Beame, who viewed the financial industry as a symbiotic partner in the great enterprise of New York City. He sought to deflect and stymie the "whispers," as he called them. But the banks' growing discomfort with the condition and character of the city's fiscal management and size of its deficits in a severe and long-lasting recession was nothing if not ominous in the middle of the recession, as New York was at the time borrowing in the short-term notes market to plug the gap between city operating expenses and tax revenues. If denied the ability to borrow to cover operating costs, the city would likely default and might well have to declare bankruptcy to shield its remaining public assets from its creditors—something no major city in the United States had ever done, and certainly not the preeminent financial and cultural capital of the nation.

Bankers were distressed, too. Many feared that the Beame administration, should the city actually default on its debt repayments obligations, might seek to pay back city employees, vendors, and welfare recipients before repaying bondholders, despite constitutional protections that called for bondholders' debts to be satisfied first. Such a sour turn of events, many believed, would severely disrupt the municipal bond market, potentially threatening the country's economic well-being and compromising the ability of many states and cities to borrow at interest rates they could reasonably afford.

As the city's financial difficulties deepened, attorneys for some banks reasoned that the financial institutions could be left legally exposed in the event of a New York City bankruptcy for having failed to disclose their knowledge of the risks and vulnerabilities they perceived about the city's financial condition—risks that prospective investors in the city's capital program had a right to know up front, before investing in New York.

So the hand-wringing and arguments went, back and forth, with the public largely unaware of it. Bond underwriting was good business, so why disrupt it, some bankers argued. The Beame administration, meanwhile, guessed that the banks' bark was worse than their bite, and anticipated stepped-up aid from Albany and Washington to keep the metropolis afloat until the recession eased, as had happened in years past.

A brief history here: Just after World War II, New York was principally a working-class city, an economic powerhouse, and the world's center of almost everything creative and new, scandalous, and wondrous. The city's plentiful factory floors and schools could, and did, accommodate the nation's poor and disenfranchised, whether they were blacks from the Jim Crow states of the South or displaced farm workers from Puerto Rico. The city had done this for the European immigrants of the nineteenth and early twentieth centuries, such as Lew and Jack Rudin's grandparents. And so it continued doing in the aftermath of World War II, as victorious veterans returned from the war by the tens of thousands, looking to jump-start the rest of their lives.

But even as people moved to New York to find work and, they hoped, decent housing (of which there was a great shortage as veterans returned), the economic landscape shifted and shriveled. Economic activity in the city's deep-water ports began to dwindle in the 1950s, as new automated technologies and freight containerization pushed the shipping industry and its jobs west to New Jersey and beyond. New interstate highways, suburbs, and growing automobile ownership projected the middle class away, along with many of their employers, large and small. The city's constellation of smaller, specialized manufacturing began to decline as well, affected by federal support to the emerging economies of the now air-conditioned South and Southwest.

Those left behind, including people facing racial barriers in moving to some of the suburbs, contended with the growing problems of unemployment, poverty, the shortage of housing, and a troubled school system serving about one million youth, most of them low-income.

Some people in the mid-1970s, including the top bankers eying city affairs nervously, sought to put all the blame for the city's predicament on Beame, though that was hardly a fair-minded analysis. Much larger forces were churning, most clearly the global recession of 1973–74, driven by the double punch of inflation and unemployment, or what the academic practitioners of the so-called dismal science—economics—termed "stagflation." The recession had been spurred by the rapid outflow of dollars as well as gold to pay for presidents Lyndon Johnson and Richard Nixon's escalation of the woefully ill-advised Vietnam War and then by the sudden and sharp rise of oil prices later brought on by the 1973 Arab oil embargo.

Not that New York's home-grown policies helped matters

much. Mayors Robert Wagner, John Lindsay, and Abe Beame successively turned to the market for short-term notes to an imprudent extent, with these higher-interest loans (which had to be paid back within a year, typically) increasing from $26 million when Wagner was mayor, to nearly $7.6 billion under Beame, the largest total by far of any city in the country. New York used this short-term borrowing to pay expenses that tax revenues were not meeting, such as employee paychecks and vendor payments, as well as to pay off short-term loans and long-term bonds as they came due for repayment with interest. It was like taking out a new credit card each month to pay down the last one.

The 1974–75 deep national recession did not cooperate with the city's timetable for the economic doldrums to lift. The downturn actually lasted far longer within the city than it did nationally, reversing the usual historic pattern. Meanwhile, property tax delinquency rose, with landlords abandoning buildings all over town to avoid overdue tax bills and utility arrears or making long-deferred repairs.

It was also true that the city and state had restrained the growth of property tax assessments for years; indeed, the average assessment slid from 82 percent of market value in 1961 to only 48 percent of market value by the mid-1970s. Some have said that the failure of successive city administrations to assess property in closer relation to its market value deprived the government of revenues when they were urgently needed.[1]

Opponents of taxation had long considered property tax increases to be a poison pill, saying that any boost in property taxes would only raise rents and chase companies away from an already highly taxed city. But the devastating cutbacks in municipal services that followed 1975, with government austerity and cutbacks, spurred at least as sizeable an exodus of businesses and population as any property tax increase could have triggered, and left the city badly positioned to fight back against a cascade of social problems to come—an epidemic of arson fires in poor neighborhoods, AIDS, the crack cocaine scourge, and the towering spike in homicides, problems that battered the city in the 1970s, '80s and '90s.[2]

Naturally, local political squabbling played a part in the drop in corporate confidence in city government in the 1970s. It was not so unusual a disagreement but it could not have been helpful when Beame clashed publicly with the city comptroller, Harrison J. Goldin, about the actual size of the city's 1975 budget deficit. In addition, a controversial practice of moving operating expenses into the capital budget, an unorthodox, stopgap accounting measure, helped obscure the seriousness of the city's budget and cash-flow vulnerabilities, effectively papering them over. Bankers and other corporate leaders questioned the financial competency of Beame and his first deputy mayor, James Cavanagh, with their old-school habits of pulling pieces of paper scribbled with numbers from their pockets when asked to define the city budget deficits or the total number of people on the city payroll. Both men, though, had reason to expect the state and federal governments would come to the city's aid, pointing out that the metropolitan region annually generated billions more in tax revenue for Washington's coffers than it got back in federal assistance.

But gratitude for the city's underlying economic strengths was hard to come by in the state and national capitals, and additional state and federal aid proved unavailing.

Lew Rudin and Jack Rudin in the U.S. Army during World War Two.
Courtesy of the Rudin family.

Lew Rudin and Mayor Ed Koch. *Courtesy of the Rudin family.*

Lew Rudin and President Ronald Reagan. *White House photograph, courtesy of the Rudin family.*

Lew Rudin and retired general and secretary of state Colin Powell. *Courtesy of the Association for a Better New York.*

Lew Rudin with, *front, left to right*: May Rudin, President George H. W. Bush; *rear, left to right:* Jack Rudin, Samantha Rudin Earls, Bill Rudin, and Rachel Rudin on the occasion of May's ninety-second birthday. *White House photograph, courtesy of the Rudin family.*

Lew Rudin and Governor Hugh Carey. *Courtesy of the Rudin family.*

Lew Rudin with Governor Mario Cuomo at an ABNY breakfast. *Courtesy of the Association for a Better New York.*

Lew Rudin playing a round of golf. *Courtesy of the Rudin family.*

Lew Rudin and former secretary of state Henry Kissinger. *Courtesy of the Rudin family.*

Lew Rudin with *(front, left to right)* former mayors John Lindsay, Abe Beame, and David Dinkins; Governor George Pataki *(rear, left)*. *Courtesy of the Association for a Better New York.*

Lew Rudin with (*left to right*) President Bill Clinton, Ophelia Rudin, Beth Rudin DeWoody, Senator Daniel Patrick Moynihan, and Rachel Rudin. *Courtesy of the Rudin Family.*

Lew Rudin and President Gerald Ford. *Courtesy of the Rudin family.*

Lew Rudin, John Cardinal O'Connor, and Jack Rudin. *Courtesy of the Rudin family.*

Lew Rudin and President Bill Clinton. *Courtesy of the Rudin family.*

Lew Rudin and Academy Award winner Sidney Poitier playing a round of golf. *Courtesy of the Rudin family.*

Lew Rudin with Nobel Peace Prize winner and president of Egypt, Anwar Sadat. *Courtesy of the Rudin family.*

Lew Rudin and U.S. Senator Alfonse D'Amato. *Courtesy of the Rudin family.*

Lew Rudin at an early ABNY board meeting with the organization's key figures including Bill Swan, Preston Robert Tisch, Alan V. Tishman, Alton Marshall, Burt French, Irving Schneider, Charles Benenson, Aaron Gural, Jerome Minskoff, Rexford Tompkins, Abraham "Bunny" Lindenbaum, and Howard Rubenstein. *Courtesy of the Rudin Family.*

Lew Rudin with Mayor Rudolph Giuliani. *Courtesy of the Rudin family.*

Lew Rudin with first lady (and future U.S. senator and secretary of state Hillary Rodham Clinton). *Courtesy of the Rudin family*

Lew Rudin with ABNY founding members Howard Rubenstein, Rexford Tompkins, Alton Marshall, and Alan Tishman. *Courtesy of the Association for a Better New York.*

Lew Rudin with Mayor John Lindsay and the ABNY board in front of Gracie Mansion. *Courtesy of the Association for a Better New York.*

Bill Rudin (*second row, center*), with (*front, left to right*) U.S. Senator John McCain, Edward Cardinal Egan, U.S. Senator (and future president) Barack Obama, and (*back row, center*) Attorney General (and future New York governor) Andrew Cuomo at the 2008 Alfred E. Smith Memorial Foundation Dinner at the Waldorf-Astoria Hotel in New York City. *Courtesy of the Rudin Family.*

Lew Rudin and his grandchildren (Carlton DeWoody, Kyle DeWoody, Samantha Rudin Earls, and Michael Rudin). *Courtesy of the Rudin family.*

Eventually, before the white-knuckle year of 1975 ended, Cavanagh submitted his resignation as first deputy mayor, a clear casualty of the lack of corporate support for the Beame administration as well as the city's reluctance, as the bankers and state officials saw it, to slash the payroll drastically enough to help bring about a balanced budget. It helped when Cavanagh was succeeded by John Zuccotti, who had been serving as chairman of the New York City Planning Commission. Zuccotti, a bright, analytical public servant who had served as an appointee of Mayor John Lindsay and who was subsequently retained by Mayor Beame, was also highly respected by business leaders and labor unions. He developed relationships with state officials in the Carey administration, such as Peter Goldmark, Richard Ravitch, Felix Rohaytn, Steven Berger, and Judah Gribetz, among others. All of these people and their colleagues were struggling to prevent New York's going into bankruptcy and to convince Washington to provide emergency aid. His relationship with Lew and Jack Rudin, as it happened, had begun many years before when he was a student and his father a maître d' at a well-known East Side watering hole called El Morocco that Jack and Lew frequented.

"He was one of those people, of whom there were only a few, who could talk to the labor people and the business people and the government leaders," Zuccotti said of Lew, who, he noticed, was quite close both to Beame and, somewhat surprisingly, to union representative and negotiator Jack Bigel as well. "He was a linkage among the three different groups that were involved, which would be the unions, the banks and the government of the City of New York. He was in sense a mediator and a facilitator."[3]

For all the efforts to keep the city from losing access to the market, it finally did when the leading bank executives of the day decided among themselves to boycott the city and no longer sell, buy, or underwrite New York City debt paper. The potential consequences of the action were anybody's guess. No one could predict what kind of impact a city bankruptcy, should it occur, would have on the faltering local or national economy, or even on the international monetary system, for which there were also fears of disruption.

In the wake of the bankers' Draconian decision, however, it appeared that a once-great city had nowhere to go but down.

7
Prepayment of Property Taxes and the Road Back to Prosperity

Then-governor Hugh Carey organized quick state support to prevent default and bankruptcy in New York City, visibly investing the state in the fate of the city. In the fall of 1975, as matters grew steadily worse and the market for a state-issued MAC bond to raise emergency capital for the city faltered and waned, Carey and the state legislature pumped more than $2 billion more into the city's coffers while at the same time establishing an emergency state fiscal control board to ride herd on the city's budget and, moreover, demonstrate to President Gerald Ford and New York's many congressional detractors that the city and state were taking pains to put their house in order, and were deserving of immediate federal seasonal loans or loan guarantees. To Carey and his talented team, the specter of a city bankruptcy was principally not only a dire threat to the city but also a clear hazard for the state government, which depended on city revenues to stay afloat and fund all the local governments and districts of the state. The economically sputtering nation would also be affected adversely by a city bankruptcy. According to the governor, it would have international economic repercussions.

President Ford, however, initially withheld support for federal aid, listening to the advice of his secretary of the treasury, William Simon, and many other White House aides such as Chief of Staff Donald Rumsfeld and Assistant Chief of Staff Dick Cheney, who succeeded Rumsfeld when the latter was appointed as secretary of defense in November 1975. Many of the president's financial regulators agreed with the recommendations of Ford's staff. He feared that many cities struggling at the time with their own finances would line up at the federal trough, and he contended that New York's politicians, and bankers, should pay the price with belt tightening for what he considered to be years of excess, citing the free tuition at the City University of New York, many employee pensions he viewed as overly generous, and far too many personnel on the city payroll.

Ford's position, which he voiced in an appearance at the National Press Club in Washington, damaged his 1976 election prospects, especially after the *New York Daily News* hit the newsstands in October 1975 with a politically devastating and instantly famous front page headline: "Ford to City: Drop Dead." The president, who was then looking ahead to a primary challenge from the more conservative Governor Ronald Reagan of California, never actually said the words "drop dead," as Ford correctly reminded Bill Rudin years later in an interview for the 2006 documentary film *The Lew Rudin Way.*[1] But Ford did say in his speech at the press club that he would oppose any aid meant to keep New York from suffering a default, other than to seek to keep "essential services" operating for New Yorkers.

Beame, angry at the banks, while furious with Washington and upset about state incursions on his budgetary powers, came to recognize the gravity of the situation as Ford and Congress deliberated the question of the city's fate. He may not have fully appreciated, though, the dramatic changes that were needed in relatively short order to win back the confidence of the striking bankers, the impersonal municipal bond market, and most Republicans and many Democrats in Washington. Beame, a graduate of City College, was a beneficiary of a liberal, pro-labor Democratic Party that rewarded party workers with civil service jobs and appointments. He now faced a crossroads in his long political career.

Some observers on the Left and Right contended that the city should go into bankruptcy rather than yield to state-led and banker-influenced incursions on its budget powers, and that a federal bankruptcy court judge would enforce a needed retrenchment more fairly. Labor leaders, though, worried about the impact of a bankruptcy on their contracts, as they thought parts would be nullified. Many conservative voices, meanwhile, called on the city to enter into a voluntary bankruptcy to get out from under union contracts, a position repeated in dozens of editorials in the *Wall Street Journal. Business Week,* required reading for many in the business community, echoed the *Journal*'s antiunion fulminations.

Lew Rudin needed no convincing that the city had to be saved from bankruptcy. Lew and Jack, like Howard Rubenstein, enjoyed many productive relationships with the trade union leaders and the municipal union movement, and were very sympathetic to both Beame and labor leaders, noting to anyone who would listen that the situation was indisputably overwhelming, and would have been for any mayor or union leader, given the many blunt demands at the time that the city slash its 330,000-person city workforce and municipal services.

Governor Carey by late August called the prospect of a city bankruptcy "unthinkable," and Rudin was among many who agreed, arguing that every effort needed to be made to keep the city out of what one columnist called "the municipal equivalent of debtor's prison." So the developer entered the fray early on—and well before things came really to a head with the famous *Daily News* headline. During the summer of 1975, as the Carey administration was organizing a "Municipal Assistance Corporation" to restructure the city's debt and stretch its repayment obligations into the future, Rudin organized some of the largest corporate property owners in town to prepay their real estate taxes for the quarterly payments due the city July 1, 1975. He also sought two additional quarterly prepayments from the corporate property owners ahead of the regular payment deadlines.

The prepayment of property taxes, when Rudin first started talking about it, was unheard of and had never been done before. Even so, he rolled out the concept and secured Beame's backing readily. Because no legal mechanism for prepayment existed, the City Charter needed to be amended—and with unprecedented speed—to allow the prepayments to flow. So the debate moved to the floor of the City Council, where it was of course contentious.

"If you want to default, just play politics," Rudin at one point warned City Council President Paul O'Dwyer and Comptroller Goldin.

"I said, *fellahs,*" Rudin later recalled, "if any of you do anything to put an obstacle in the way of this bill, there will not be one cent paid in prepayment of taxes, and the city will default." And he was not exaggerating: the city might well have defaulted that summer. "If you want the city to survive," he added, "this is I think the way, at least for now."[2]

The City Charter amendment was accomplished in record

time, and the bill that Rudin inspired and lobbied for frantically was signed that June. The first round of tax prepayments arrived in August. Over three quarters in all, the prepayment of taxes provided a total of $600 million from Con Edison, New York Telephone, the New York Bank for Savings, New York Life, and of course, Rudin Management and other major property owners in the city. The method was renewed in 1977 at the request of Mayor Koch to ease the impact of continuing budget gaps.

In return for the advances, the participating businesses received interest payments worth 8 percent on their "loans" to their city government. While the property owners were thus compensated and rewarded, the entire episode marked one of Rudin's most memorable feats. Without the bill, "we would have gone down," speculated Felix Rohatyn, looking back at the situation facing the city in the summer of 1975, during an interview in 2012.[3]

"Nobody likes to pay taxes," former governor Carey, who died in 2011, mused years after the crisis, "least of all landlords. So Lew got them all together and said 'Do you know what we're going to do? We're not going to wait for the bill. We're going to take next year's taxes and pay them now. That way the city will get cash flow which will ward off the creditors.' Now, was it a small thing? No," the former governor went on. "Lew had to change the law to get the city to accept their money. Where did he get the time? Where did he get the will? I think it came from a love of New York. A real devotion to the city. People like Lew saved New York,"[4] said the governor, who was called by many "the man who saved New York."

Walter Wriston of First National City Bank (later Citibank), although philosophically bonded to ideas of small government and a free market economy, decided in the fall of 1975 to join forces with the Carey administration, Republican State Senate Majority Leader Warren Anderson, and Senate Democratic leader Manfred Ohrenstein and even Beame in mobilizing political support for federal aid. That October, Wriston testified to a congressional panel that while he believed the economic impact of a city bankruptcy was "containable, with some trauma," Washington should provide the city with federal bond guarantees to avoid what he called a real potential for urban riots, looting and other social upheaval from "no police, no firemen, no welfare workers."[5] The conservative Treasury Secretary Simon, who spearheaded the Ford administration's opposition to federal aid and assailed the city's social democratic traditions, commented at the time that listening to Wriston's testimony represented "the saddest day of my life."[6]

Speaking later of Rudin's prepayment accomplishment in the summer of 1975, Wriston called it a memorable stroke of salesmanship. "To persuade a real estate fellow to pay his taxes ahead of time is an act of salesmanship that is quite remarkable, believe me," the banker said after retiring from the bank. "And he achieved it somehow."[7] Senator Ohrenstein echoed these remarks and even said, "Lew Rudin was the key New York City civic leader who was involved in developing a coalition of business leaders, community figures and New York state and city elected officials in preventing bankruptcy in New York."[8]

The prepayment initiative was the first of many important fiscal improvisations that New York officials initiated throughout the year until, finally, Ford relented in December under growing domestic and international pressure from New York Governor Hugh Carey, Vice President Nelson Rockefeller, as well as from West Germany's Chancellor Helmut Schmidt and France's President Valery Giscard d'Estaing, among others. With as little fanfare as imaginable, Ford signed a bill giving the city $2.3 billion in seasonal loans, all paid back at a profit to the Treasury compared to the going interest rates. The loans were approved by Ford and Congress only after the Carey administration had restructured the city's debt, imposed an emergency fiscal control board on the city's budgetary autonomy, laid off tens of thousands of city workers, and even approved a stay on repayment of debt principal to holders of city bonds (later overturned as unconstitutional).

Even as he sought to assist the Carey and Beame administrations in slashing city spending to avoid bankruptcy and engender Congressional support for federal aid, Lew Rudin never seemed to lose sight of the impact of the city's lasting austerity program and budget cuts on neighborhoods, where the effects were devastating, said former city Teamsters local president Barry Feinstein in a 2002 interview.

"There were guidance counselors laid off, there were gym classes canceled as the teacher ranks shrunk because of layoffs," Feinstein recalled, "and many programs were eliminated to do the more basic kind of education. Lew thought this was terrible and put together a program to fund activities that had been eliminated by the Board of Education as a result of funding shortages, and he was able to be responsible for putting back into play afterschool programs that had been ended. That's how Lew thought about what New York needed."[9]

Much like Carey, Rudin was instrumental in selling a larger idea that remains relevant, which Wriston referred to as "'burden sharing' . . . that is, whether it was labor, capital or real estate, everybody was taking less than the market rate for something" in order to prevent an eventuality—bankruptcy—that would have been damaging to everyone."[10] Rudin arrived earlier than most citizens or elected officials at the fiscal crisis barricades and fought effectively in favor of keeping the city afloat. He also made trips throughout that tense fall and winter to the Capitol to help city and state elected and business leaders lobby for federal aid, bringing recognizable New Yorkers like former Miss America Bess Myerson to press the case for their beleaguered hometown. As the crisis gathered force, and as public anger and protests rose over sharp city cutbacks, Rudin arranged private meetings with Felix Rohatyn, Jack Bigel, and Barry Feinstein, among others, helping to ensure that labor, finance, and government continued to work out their differences and work together.

"He was New York's unofficial ambassador," said Alton Marshall.[11]

Nevertheless, the slow, arduous climb back from near-bankruptcy transpired over many difficult and fractious years in New York. In the summer of 1977, for example, a bolt of lightning touched off a citywide blackout, leading to uncontrollable looting in the darkness and scorching heat. In the late 1970s, many New Yorkers probably felt the city's best days were past. Others termed the town just too anarchic to be governable. Clearly, the civic fabric was tested as library branches and firehouses shuttered and people and businesses fled. The subway fare leaped from thirty-five to fifty cents in the middle of hard times for working people and the unemployed. A nearly completed hospital in Brooklyn sat vacant, the capital funds unavailable to finish it. About 340,000 jobs disappeared between 1973 and 1976, with more to come. Felonies reached record heights. Commercial construction ground to a near-halt. In many ways that were undeniable, New York was approaching rock bottom.

The Rudins stayed in the city and challenged the conventional notion of the city's imminent and inevitable demise, always appreciating its capacity for reinvention, a natural process the fiscal crisis merely interrupted. Things were not all bad, Lew was quick to point out.

What was happening in many parts of the struggling city, at least for those who cared to look with a certain degree of faith and hopefulness, was in some sense a testament to the city's original and resilient character. Though still barely detectable, new waves of immigrants from the Caribbean, Latin America, Asia, Africa, and the Middle East were arriving and reinventing neighborhoods throughout the city, the gates having been flung wide open by the progressive 1965 immigration law signed in front of the Statue of Liberty by President Lyndon Johnson.

In the late 1970s, however, one still needed an awful lot of bullishness, which Rudin had, to see past the recession and rampant social ills to the horizon of a better future, or even to see through Hollywood's popular vigilante fantasies such as the *Death Wish* series (starting in 1974) and *Taxi Driver* (1976). Though Jimmy Carter's inauguration of 1977 came within months of the coming New York City blackout, and amidst the collapsing condition of the South Bronx, which became a national symbol of urban distress, New York City was still considered the nation's cultural and financial capital, and many international companies still wanted to do business in and with it. Rudin sought to strengthen the city's reputation as a destination for business at all times. One such example was when he came out strongly in favor of allowing the new supersonic Concorde to land at Kennedy Airport, in spite of opposition from Queens communities near the airport whose residents objected to the explosive report of the 1,350 mile an hour aircraft's sonic boom as it came in for a landing.

Rudin believed that the city, and America, needed the high-speed transatlantic connection and its first-class travelers, and he volunteered to help the European companies and government supporters plead their case to the city and state. Nonetheless, the Port Authority of New York, which had jurisdiction over the airport, banned the jet for a period of time, heeding the concerns of middle-class neighborhoods adjacent to JFK, including Howard Beach. His position in many ways was similar to his stance in favor of Westway, a proposed West Side highway construction project that supporters believed would benefit the city's economy, but whose detractors argued could only be done at the expense of mass transit aid, and was liable, too, to be environmentally harmful by opening the way for more automobile traffic on the West Side.

From European leaders came dismay at the Port Authority's seeming provinciality in the face of a new and promising advance such as the supersonic jet, or what the jet's supporters called the "myopia" of airport-adjacent Queens neighborhoods like Howard Beach. Many Concorde supporters downplayed the noise that adjacent communities might hear. "The airport is on the sea, and the sea is crowded by fish, not by people," said an incredulous French president Valery Giscard d'Estaing.[12]

Rudin agreed. "I just couldn't see how New York City could tell all the important business people of the world to go to Boston or Washington on the Concorde and not come to the City of New York," he said, remembering the drawn-out battle in the wake of the fiscal crisis.[13]

After his efforts to secure the Concorde's landing rights, Lew was made an honorary Officer of the Most Excellent Order of the British Empire (OBE) by the British Government in 1979.[14]

Ultimately, a federal judge, Milton Pollack, ruled the futuristic plane could land at JFK on a test basis, and the U.S. Supreme Court in 1977 refused to overturn the lower court's decision, thus ending the Port Authority ban. First test-flown in 1969, the Concorde thus resumed its commercial flights to New York, continuing them on and off until July 2000 after a fatal crash in Paris—which ended the entire matter.

8
New York City Marathon

When, in the fall of 2012, Hurricane Sandy blacked out most of Manhattan south of Fortieth Street and caused widespread devastation in coastal areas of the city and the region, the Bloomberg administration was reluctant, at first, to cancel the New York Marathon, a race that annually filled the streets of the five boroughs with tens of thousands of runners and millions of spectators. Many police officers and firefighters who were desperately needed elsewhere were in no mood to stand watch over a daylong race winding through many suffering coastal neighborhoods.

The mayor's refusal drew outrage from the *New York Post,* whose front-page headline read "Abuse of Power," and whose editorial page called for the mayor to cancel the event. The *New York Times* and the *New York Daily News* and almost all other local media agreed.

Initially, Bloomberg considered green-lighting the race even as thousands of people were still without power or heat and reeling from the flooding and destruction of their homes and communities. The mayor did finally cancel the race amid the public outcry, as he should have, even considering that his initial motives for wanting to preserve the scheduled marathon were well intentioned. In 2001, the marathon, organized by the New York Road Runners Club, had gone off on schedule, less than two months after the destruction of the World Trade Center by terrorists, and may well have served as a partial balm for the badly wounded city.

Back in the 1970s, though, no one could have imagined that the marathon would carry so much significance for the entire city when it was run only within Central Park. No one, that is, except perhaps Lew and Jack Rudin, and a few others who sensed its untapped worth as a vehicle for civic pride and promotion.

The notion of a *citywide* marathon to supplant the race that had always been run inside the pastoral confines of Central Park was first advanced by Percy Sutton, the liberal Democratic attorney and Manhattan borough president who hoped to win the upcoming 1977 Democratic mayoral primary, for which there was an unusually large field. George Spitz, an assistant to the speaker of the Assembly when Sutton had been a member of the Assembly, was a former marathon runner who turned to Sutton one day and said, "Why don't we take the marathon out of Central Park"—where it looped several times to make a 26.2 mile circuit—"and out into all five boroughs of the city?"[1]

"I didn't know where I was going to raise the money," Sutton recalled years later. "But we said we would try to raise the money for it, and I insisted that we touch all of the major cultural areas [in New York City]—that is, we would go through a Polish community, we'd go through a Jewish community, we'd go through an Italian community, a Hispanic community, a black community, a Chinese community." And in his office high in the Municipal Building across the street from City Hall, Sutton began to chart the route the race might take.

While Sutton had supported Beame back in 1973, the

mayor and the cash-strapped city were in no position to underwrite the borough president's concept, nor were the marathon's organizers, the New York Road Runners Club. Still, Sutton went to see Beame and on the way out of the meeting he saw Jack and Lew entering City Hall. "And I said to them, 'I've got something for you.'

"I've just promised the mayor that I can raise the money," he went on, "and we need twenty-five thousand dollars to start the marathon and it's going to be the biggest thing you've ever seen," Sutton told them. "Lew said yeah, I've got to talk to Jack, and he talked to Jack." And he came back with a promise to invest the needed $25,000 that was requested. Eric Rudin, Jack Rudin's son, later said, "It was going to be done one time in nineteen seventy-six in honor of the bicentennial and that was it. It was supposed to be a one-shot deal, and Jack and Lewis said, 'Well, we'll do it. We'll give you the twenty-five thousand, but we'd like to have the trophy named in honor of our late father (my grandfather), Sam Rudin, who was a long distance runner.' "[2]

"It's now known all over the world as the greatest marathon of all, because of a guy named Sam Rudin and his two sons named Lewis and Jack Rudin," Sutton marveled.

The Rudins' financing allowed the marathon to become a signature New York sporting event that today draws tens of thousands of runners and many more tourists. Lew became the event's honorary chairman.

Not too many people were interested in the change at first. When Percy Sutton first announced the decision to take the 1976 marathon citywide, only one reporter showed up at the press conference, Howard Rubenstein remembered. Lew and Jack then asked for his help with promotion. "It was during

Abe Beame's administration," said Rubenstein. "I lined up all the members of the Board of Estimate in Central Park and we ran a hundred-yard dash to kick off the new marathon. I thought it would kill some of those guys. They had never walked fast, forget run. But that was the beginning of our promotion of the marathon. What an opportunity it was for me. What a wonderful thing Lew and Jack contributed to New York."[3]

The once-modest marathon, whose first race in 1970 included but 127 participants, grew to 47,000 finishers, with up to two million cheering spectators, and 315 million viewers watching on television worldwide—a huge media spectacle. It drummed up business for airlines, hotels, restaurants, street vendors, and merchants, showcasing the city in a broad and positive way to the nation and the world. In the end, the marathon became what Rubenstein called a "unifying force" for the city's many proud multicultural neighborhoods, and for the city as a whole.

9
International Tennis Becomes Synonymous with New York

Late in 1976, Rudin received a phone call. The voice on the other end of the line had a distinct Southern accent. He didn't recognize it, nor had he ever met the man calling.

"Hah there, Lew," the voice drawled, "Ah'm Slew—Slew Hester. Just call me Slew!"[1]

Hester, an oil wildcatter from Mississippi, was the head of the U.S. Tennis Association. Someone had suggested he get in touch with the well-connected real estate developer, and fast. He told Rudin he was planning to pull the U.S. Open out of the privately run West Side Tennis Club, its home for six decades in Forest Hills, Queens, and move it to another state if necessary—unless, that is, someone in the city could provide an up-to-date venue within New York City, his preferred location.

The USTA contract with the West Side Tennis Club was going to run out in 1978, and the association's brash president had told the trustees of the venerable private club that the 1977 Open was going to be the last one ever held in their antiquated stadium in Forest Hills. He had already rejected their sole offer, given its insistence that the USTA pay as much as $7 million—money it did not have—to expand and renovate the 14,000-seat arena, with its inadequate parking, faded locker rooms, and sweltering clubhouse. The West Side Tennis Club also wanted a heavy share of future profits.[2]

Hester already had an idea about where to move. On a commercial plane circling to land at LaGuardia Airport, he had peered out the portal and noticed an aging structure—the abandoned Louis Armstrong Stadium. The former "Singer Bowl," renamed for the great jazz musician, who lived in nearby Corona, was a rusted relic of the 1964 World's Fair and looked deteriorated even from three thousand feet up.

Hester asked Rudin: Does anyone think that the stadium could be revamped in time for the 1978 U.S. Open championship a little more than a year and a half away?

Rudin had no idea. He might well have thought to himself, "Are you kidding? In New York?" But he offered the caller the names of three or four architects who might be willing to sketch a quick site plan for the decrepit arena in Flushing Meadows Park.

All the same, the idea appealed to Rudin, and he grew more and more involved, running interference for the brash out-of-towner at the mayor's office, the parks department, the Board of Estimate, and many bureaucratic agencies, and among local and state office holders who had a stake in the outcome of what was billed as the largest public project of the time, but who held differing views about how and whether it should or could be accomplished.

The only architect to answer Hester's call that same sunny, cold Friday afternoon when Hester phoned Rudin was a relatively little-known but experienced architect, David Kenneth Specter. Hester, a man who trusted his own instincts, showed up at Specter's office about a half-hour after reaching him, chomping on his nearly ever-present cigar. After a quick look at his portfolio of architectural blueprints, he signed Specter up.

Specter soon realized he had agreed to perform a Herculean task, as the arena would need to be rebuilt in record time, and from scratch, and needed all the many necessary government permits and approvals. Blithely unaware of the structural and political obstacles that awaited, he put together a diagrammatic site plan in two days, and the city quickly followed suit, putting the city-owned arena out for bid. None of the proposals came close to the USTA offer.

The terms were described by Specter in an article he later wrote in *Tennis Week* about the project, the most memorable of his professional career for its rapid-fire execution and its public importance. In exchange for leasing sixteen acres in the sprawling public park, the USTA agreed to spend at least $5 million on a new tennis center seating 26,500 people (the figure would grow to $10 million). The association was to receive exclusive use of the site and its revenues for, at most, sixty days a year for fifteen years. USTA would operate and maintain the tennis center year-round as a public facility, paying New York City ten percent of the court rental fees or an annual minimum of $125,000, whichever was greater.[3] The city also was eligible to receive about $175,000 each year from parking fees from tennis center patrons at the adjacent, city-owned Shea Stadium, and a fifty-fifty split on rental fees and food and beverage receipts for non-USTA events such as rock concerts.

Slew Hester did not ask for any public financing for fear of slowing things down. But he did exclude the city from receiving any portion of the U.S. Open's major revenue sources, such as pricey admission fees and food concessions.

The terms of the deal were reported in the press during the public phase of the approval process, but some were troubled by the quasi-private use of city parkland, and others were simply suspicious of the latest grandiose-sounding city development scheme. But the construction worker unions and electrician unions wanted the deal for the hundreds of construction jobs it augured; newspapers supported it; and reporters covering the story found in Slew Hester a good ol' boy—who stood out in New York—that they liked to cover.

In less than two years from the time Hester first phoned Rudin out of the blue and picked an architect, and after many seemingly insoluble design challenges were overcome, on August 28, 1978, the first tennis ball was in play before twenty thousand fans, in the dramatically reconfigured arena. Within four years, the USTA paid off the Citibank loan for the stadium renovation, which had been secured with revenues from its television contract with CBS. It was a lucrative deal for the tennis education and promotion association, yielding a reported net annual profit of about $50 million.

When, in 1993, the stadium lease with the city expired. Lew again got involved to keep the U.S. Open in New York. Mayor Dinkins and his administration gave invaluable support by allowing the USTA to build a new and larger main stadium at the National Tennis Center site. Arthur Ashe Stadium opened in 1997 under a new ninety-nine-year lease between the city and the USTA for the 46.5 acre site. The USTA pays a base rent of $400,000, plus 1 percent of its gross revenues, including the admission tickets bought by hundreds of thousands, television earnings, and concessions such as the event's $10 hamburgers. The new lease has generated an average of $2 million a year for New York City, according to the USTA.

Mayor Michael Bloomberg would come to call it "the only good athletic sports stadium deal, not just in New York, but in the country." Financing for the new stadium was provided by $250 million in New York City Industrial Development Bonds.[4]

In addition to pointing to the role played by Slew Hester, George Gowen, who was USTA's general counsel at the time of the original deal, recalled Lew Rudin's involvement as similarly crucial. Whether Rudin anticipated the enormous success of the Open—and he was supportive of David Dinkins's important negotiations over the ninety-nine-year lease, despite vocal opposition by candidate and later mayor Rudy Giuliani—Rudin's instincts about the project's potentially enduring value for the city's economy and promotion proved accurate.[5]

"I think that the tennis center is a great tribute to Lew," commented Jon Tisch, chairman of Loews Hotels (and Bob Tisch's son), when he looked back at the 1970s project debate and the 1990s reprise, in an interview. "Without him working with the people, with the tennis people, we wouldn't have this magnificent facility, which bring in two weeks of great attention and business to the city every year, in addition to what it does for the youngsters who use it all during the year. This great Arthur Ashe Stadium would not be there unless Lew had interceded and mediated, between the USTA and the city political forces. It's a great tribute to him that it was accomplished."[6]

The U.S. Open became one of the premier sporting events in the country. As former mayor Dinkins—principal proponent of the stadium lease's late-1993 revisions and renewal—noted, and as Ed Koch's and Michael Bloomberg's subsequent positive appraisals reflected, the city's revenues from the stadium well exceeded the city' annual revenues from its other stadium leases with the Yankees and the Mets.[7] The USTA pays all maintenance costs and it also makes the facility available to the public eight months each year. The development of the stadium and its leases were "living proof," one reviewer, Julia Vitullo Martin, wrote in the *New York Sun* in 2003, "that a public-private partnership can pay off in immense public benefits that couldn't be won by either sector alone."[8] Here was an instance of Rudin's vision, writ large.

Apart from its revenue stream and marketing value for the city, the city recently estimated that the U.S. Open generates $756 million in both directly related and indirect economic activities, noting, too, that it takes place during a slow season for hotels and restaurants and draws an unusually high percentage of visitors, and celebrities, from out of state and outside the country. Attendance topped 700,000 in 2012, while on television and through various media, the U.S. Open attracted a reported eighty-five million television viewers in the United States. It is also broadcast in 188 countries, at last count.

"It began with a Southern boy who could charm the birds out of the trees, and with Lew Rudin, whose only interest was benefitting the City of New York—his real estate interests weren't going to be improved by what happened in Queens—and who just had a real love of New York throughout his life," said Gowen, the former USTA counsel.[9]

10
Protecting Local and State Tax Deductions

The city was on its way back, its economy improving, when one spring day in 1985, U.S. Senator Alfonse D'Amato of New York invited, via an urgently worded mailgram, hundreds of the wealthiest and most important business executives in the city to a meeting at a Manhattan hotel, where he warned them that the second Reagan administration was proposing to overhaul the national tax code and that its most troublesome provision for New York was the proposed elimination of the tax deduction for local and state taxes.

The Reagan tax reform initiative had been kicking around for more than a year and its latest configuration "involved the largest corporate tax increase in history and the most drastic crackdown on loopholes for the affluent," political reporter Albert R. Hunt later wrote in the introduction to a 1987 book about the epic battle to overhaul the tax code, *Showdown at Gucci Gulch,* by journalists Jeffrey H. Birnbaum and Alan S. Murray.[1]

As unpopular as so much of the bill was with D'Amato's audience that day, it was over the deductibility provision's elimination that he sought to mobilize New York's business elite, to work with him on Capitol Hill to oppose it, saying it threatened to send the wealthiest New Yorkers packing for lower-taxed regions and to make attracting and retaining corporations more difficult. The senator said the bill was gaining momentum in Congress and had drawn support from both Democratic Representative Dan Rostenkowski, the chairman of the House Ways and Means Committee, and Republican Senator Bob Packwood, chairman of the Senate Finance Committee. Both leaders saw the tax code as a potentially historic feat and a way to achieve a variety of economic and social goals.

Speaking to about two hundred bankers, developers, and corporate executives, D'Amato said that "this was going to be terrible for the city and we have to do something," remembered Jay Kriegel, who was there, "and we've got to mobilize, and we need someone to head up the campaign. And Jimmy Robinson [of American Express] spoke up and said, 'Yep, Lew Rudin is going to do this for us. I think Lew Rudin is the perfect person to do this.'"[2]

Kriegel was standing in the back of the room at the time, and Lew Rudin immediately called over to him and said, "What the hell am I going to do?" He couldn't say no, even if he wanted to. And he didn't.

Soon, Rudin and the perceptive Kriegel, who signed on as the chief counsel of the pushback, brought in former New York Republican senator Jacob Javits as the lead Washington lobbyist. Together, they led one of the most high-powered, well-financed, and persistent lobbying campaigns that Washington had ever seen in an effort to preserve the tax deductibility provision.

Backed by a Who's Who of leading business figures and elected officials from New York and California, Rudin, Kriegel, and Javits made a brash, deft end run around the powerful

Ways and Means Committee chairman Rostenkowski, winning over most of the members of the committee—the House tax-writing panel—to the merits of leaving the deductibility provision in place. "We beat him in his own committee, which was not easily done," recalled Kriegel, mentioning in particular that Rep. Martin Russo of Illinois, a Rostenkowski protégé (and, serendipitously enough, the Washington roommate of then Democratic Brooklyn congressman Charles Schumer), proved one of the most helpful to the New Yorkers in turning the tables on Rostenkowski, who had delivered a speech on national television supporting the Reagan tax bill despite many reservations in his own party. Russo "stuck his neck out for us," Kriegel said, adding that the then relatively little-known governor from Arkansas named Bill Clinton also strongly supported the New Yorkers' cause from early on, and helped in making it into a national issue.[3]

To the White House chief of staff Donald Regan, the deductibility provision was, throughout the debate, an essential means of keeping the tax code reform "revenue neutral," the goal professed by President Reagan amid fierce popular outcry against both taxes and tax loopholes, notably in his home state of California. Echoing some of President Ford's arguments about New York during the 1975 fiscal crisis, President Reagan's chief of staff argued for repealing the deduction, saying that states that chose to provide better or more services ought not be rewarded with a federal tax break in the form of local and state tax deductibility. Governor Cuomo responded, however, that New York performed a number of functions he described as essentially federal responsibility, such as drug enforcement and providing medical care for poor and undocumented immigrants.

"I remember the two of us, Lew and I, went to visit with the secretary of the treasury, Jim Baker at that time, to talk about that particular issue, and the political message we were given was that the administration intended to ride the unpopularity of New York to get that provision put in place, and that we were fighting a losing cause," said James Robinson III of American Express. "We tried to make it clear, and Lew was quite passionate in his statements, that this was not just a local issue, but an issue in almost every community around the country, and we were going to carry that message broadly and widely and frequently, which we did through ABNY and thorough other coalitions that we put together."[4]

When the Tax Reform Act of 1986 was signed into law in October, it simplified the income tax code, broadened the tax base, and eliminated many tax shelters and other preferences that had so infuriated many Americans. The president's goal of revenue neutrality for the bill was targeted by decreasing individual tax rates, eliminating $30 billion annually in loopholes, and increasing corporate taxes. While the bill reduced the number of deductions and tax brackets drastically, it did not repeal local and state tax deductions.

During the debate, the New York lobby, including Kriegel, pointedly reminded senators and potential presidential candidates, leaders such as Al Gore and George Mitchell, that they had gotten a lot of campaign contributions from business leaders and wealthy individuals of New York City. "So you came up to New York, where all this money is, and we expect some support for New York," was what Kriegel remembered telling—at times yelling—at senators. Kriegel added, "I pretty much screamed at them so that Lew wouldn't have to." Rudin, he noted, was more conciliatory by nature, and did not really hold grudges.[5] Reflecting the intensity of the debate, Gov. Mario Cuomo, who also felt strongly about the local-tax deduction issue, told a gathering of contributors to the Democratic Senate Campaign Committee in May 1985 that he would not help out-of-state congressional candidates raise money in New York if they opposed the state's position against eliminating the deductibility provision from the tax code.[6]

Rudin never forgot the entire episode, which had brought to the fore his unmatched networking prowess. At one point, when the final terms of the tax overhaul bill were becoming clearer, he had a memorable close encounter with President Reagan and some of his top advisors during a visit to the West Coast.

"I was a member of the Executive Committee to raise funds for construction of the Reagan library in Simi Valley, California, and we'd go down three times a year to the White House for lunch to hear how the fundraising was going," Rudin recalled, late in life. "I was sitting next to President Reagan and Attorney General Edwin Meese and chief of staff Don Regan, whom I'd known and who was an old friend of mine since the time that he chaired Merrill Lynch and we worked on a business-labor task force set up by David Rockefeller and [trade union leader] Harry Van Arsdale. Regan turned to me and said, 'Well, you beat us at Ways and Means. But we're still going to get you real estate guys.' And he did,"[7] said Rudin.

Among other things Rudin felt were harmful was the approved bill's elimination of sales tax deductibility (restored only in 2005 under the American Job Creation Act of 2004), as well as changes in the depreciation schedule, which blunted property owners' ability to write off their commercial investments on a pro-rated basis.

Within a year of the bill's signing, the stock market and the savings and loan industry collapsed and the real estate business "went into the tank," said Rudin, who blamed some of the tax policies instituted in the Reagan years. The harsh downturn, which battered the city's real estate industry, lasted into the mid-1990s. Yet, in time, the city eventually managed to shake off the doldrums. Washington's "trickle-down" tax policies and the deregulation gathered steam in the mid-2000s, fueling huge investments, and sky-high gains, in the equities markets.

With that deluge of wealth came the tech bubble, the credit boom, the derivatives boom, and of course the real estate bubble. While this overheating of the economy would lead to the global financial economic meltdown of 2007–08, it enriched the Big Apple, home of Wall Street, of course, and a disproportionately large share of the nation's wealth and power. The rise of so much affluence drove the real estate industry to record heights of profit never before seen, and Rudin Management's profits from renting luxury apartments and premium office space only soared.

To the extent that Rudin's pro–real estate viewpoints attracted critics as the city became less affordable to people with average incomes in the heady years leading up to the 2007–08 worldwide economic crisis, it could have been due in part to his long-time, unswerving opposition to state laws that protected tenants from sudden rent spikes or eviction. Michael McKee, a long-time tenants advocate in the city, recalled that Lew seemed to take it personally when, more than once, they clashed in televised discussions on the issue of rent regulations, including in 1997, after Joseph Bruno, the Republican majority leader of the New York State Senate, led a legislative effort, supported by the real estate industry, to let the city's rent stabilization law expire. McKee and other advocates for tenants contended that the action would lead to quick evictions of tens of thousands of lower-income, lower-paying tenants, even though he felt that the Rudins were not the type of landlords to mistreat tenants or put them on the street.

"Someone moving to New York today, if they find anywhere to live at all, it'll be a market-rate apartment. And the market rate is something most New Yorkers can't afford," said McKee.[8]

The Rudin family and many other people, however, maintained that Lew's allegiance to the city's overall well-being was broad and deep, and extended well beyond any notion of class or the largely affluent clientele who rented his apartments. Indeed, since many people knew of Beth Rudin DeWoody's specialty in the arts and her father's understanding of the economic impact through tourism that the arts have on New York City, they thought that he would be honored to be called a patron of the arts and "a collector of art." However, Lew corrected some of these people, saying, "More important to me are people, and if I collect anything, I collect people," she said.

"He loved people, and working with people in different social classes," Beth said. "His friends not only included the President of the U.S., but taxi drivers and sanitation workers." Indeed, he surprised many of his colleagues by supporting the city's garbage men when they demanded a higher salary from the city, or even when they went on strike. He believed that they deserved a higher salary for the important and necessary work they shouldered. [9]

At the same time, Rudin felt strongly that the federal government should not provide too many tax deductions, or loopholes, and that everyone, including the wealthy, should pay their fair share rather than seek ever-inventive ways to avoid their civic onus. He opposed state taxation, suggesting that state levies should be replaced by federal taxation whenever possible, based on each individual's income level. This would be fairer, he contended, to lower- and middle-class New Yorkers forced to shoulder local, state, and federal burdens.

11
A Living Landmark

Although Lew Rudin suffered from glaucoma most of his adult life and progressively lost his eyesight, when it came to New York, he had true 20/20 vision for what was needed to make his great city even better.

"Lew had been diagnosed with glaucoma for quite some time," recalled Ophelia Rudin, Lew's daughter-in-law. "He would be standing next to you and wasn't really sure sometimes who you were. He had a definite physiological vision issue. But the point is, Lew always saw better than anybody else."[1]

There is no doubt that throughout Lew's life, he was able to see challenges and opportunities coming; he would see who could help, and he could encourage those interests to come to bear on the problem with him. Lew was a visionary until the day he died.

Rudin's friend Martin Berger, a New York housing and office developer from Westchester County, said of him, "He was a man of integrity. He was obviously one of the most powerful men in New York. He really never used that power for self-gain or aggrandizement. He was very careful about it. It was very interesting: he would never get involved in a project in New York where his access to public officials would assist him in getting an edge. He was very sensitive about these things, and I really admired that."[2]

Lew, in his final days was always surrounded by his loved ones—family and friends. He greeted a steady stream of prominent visitors who came from all over the country to be with him. They included Bill and Hillary Clinton, Art and Pat Modell from Baltimore, Ira and Nicki Harris from Florida, Howard Rubenstein and Judge Burton Roberts from New York, and the leaders of government from both political parties and the captains of industry. They were losing someone with whom they had worked with, a good guy, a straight shooter, and above all, a friend.

Howard Rubenstein, his longtime friend and close associate at the Association for a Better New York, remembered Rudin's last words with him shortly before he died: "Take care of New York."[3]

Many people have spoken since Lew's death about the similarities between Lew Rudin and his son Bill and their common energy and drive in attempting to aid New York and make it a better city for all its residents.

One of them was Randi Weingarten, president of the American Federation of Teachers, the featured speaker at an ABNY breakfast meeting in the spring of 2013. She had been president of the United Federation of Teachers in New York when Lew was alive and after Bill succeeded him. In her address, she began by stating how similar Bill was to his father, given their personal and public commitments, civic involvement, and their great desire to improve New York.[4] Michelle Adams, a former executive director of ABNY, in an interview, spoke too of Bill's and Lew's "common DNA," which she believed had to be the same because of the many similarities they exhibited in their lives.[5] Rachel Rudin, Lew's widow, said father and son spoke and thought alike.[6] Vicki Lurie, who worked for both Lew and Bill Rudin over a period of three decades, noted that "[Lew] was passionate about New York City. He had a mission and cared very deeply for those who lived in the city," as well as for those who work in the city.[7] Kenneth Langone, a co-founder of Home Depot remarked of Bill, "Apples don't fall far from the tree. He had a good mentor and a good coach in his father and Uncle Jack, It was hard to go off the track with that kind of inspiration and influence in his life. It was impossible."[8]

More than a decade after Lew's death, Bill Rudin talked at length about his father in the company's office at 345 Park Avenue. One could already see a tangible sign of recovery from the 9/11 attacks: One World Trade Center downtown was on its way toward completion, climbing skyward where the Twin Towers once stood, and the World Trade Center memorial to the victims of 9/11 had opened and become one of the city's most poignant and moving monuments. Bill, along with his uncle, Jack, cousin, Eric, and sister, Beth, and with the next generation not too far behind, now lead the company. Bill and Ophelia's son, Michael, and daughter, Samantha, are both actively engaged in the family business, as well as the city's philanthropic causes. Beth, in fact, often speaks proudly of the five generations of Rudin family involvement in New York real estate.[9] In 2012, Samantha gave birth to Elle. Only time will tell whether the infant will eventually become involved in the family business. Meanwhile, under Bill's leadership, the Association for a Better New York continues its regular breakfast meetings involving public policy and civic improvement issues.

Thankfully, Bill said, Lew never had to see what the enemies of New York and America had wrought on 9/11 shortly before he died, though he knew that some kind of calamity had befallen his city.

What would he have done had he been alive and healthy?

"Are you kidding?" Bill said. "He'd have been the first to go down there and say we are going to rebuild and make it better than it was before."[10]

Just look at this great city, Lew Rudin might well have said had he witnessed the smoldering ruins, in much the same way that he expressed determination and hope in the face of the city's worst recessions, fiscal crises, and political and social challenges during the course of his eventful and civically engaged lifetime.

You cannot ever replicate or replace this great city, he might well have continued. So, never give up on New York. Work together, work out your differences, and above all, strive to make the city better than it is!

That was precisely what Lew Rudin did best.

And for that reason—not his buildings, connections, or wealth — he deserves to be remembered.

Notes

1. "Take Care of Our City"

1. Family members recalled the funeral to the author, and newspaper coverage was also helpful. Lew Rudin's last days and funeral were depicted by Bill Rudin (interview with the author, Dec. 10, 2012); Charles Bagli, "Lewis Rudin, Head of Real Estate Family and Frequent City Fiscal Savior, Dies at 74," *New York Times*, Sept. 21, 2001; Clem Richardson, "VIPs eulogize 'Mr. N.Y.,'" *New York Daily News*, Sept. 24, 2001; Carter B. Horsley, "Lew Rudin Memorial Service," thecityreview.com, Sept. 24, 2001.
2. Jay Kriegel, interviewed by the author and Robert Polner, New York, NY, Sept. 20, 2012.
3. Bill Rudin,interviewed by the author and Robert Polner, New York, NY, Dec. 10, 2012.
4. Ibid.
5. Richardson, "VIPs eulogize 'Mr. N.Y.'"
6. Ibid.
7. Ibid.
8. Ibid.
9. Robert Kolker, "City Father's Son," *New York,* Sept. 11, 2002.
10. Fred R. Paprin (New York University alumnus, who attended the Marxism class), telephone interview by Robert Polner, Dec. 20, 2012.
11. Edward I. Koch, interview by the author, New York, NY, Oct. 11, 2012.

12. Betsy Gotbaum, telephone interview by Robert Polner, Jan. 8, 2013.
13. Jack Rudin, Susan Rudin, and Lori Barclay, interview by the author and Robert Polner, New York, NY, Oct. 12, 2012
14. Henry Kissinger, interview by the author and Robert Polner, New York, NY, Nov. 26, 2012.
15. Bill Rudin, interview.
16. Bagli, "Lewis Rudin, Head of Real Estate Family."

2. Family Roots

1. Jack Rudin, interview by John Emmerling in *The Rudin Family of New York: Featuring Jack Rudin*, directed by John Emmerling (New York: 2004), DVD.
2. Property records at New York City Department of Finance, Manhattan Business Center, Office of the City Register.
3. The author's understanding of Louis Rudinsky's background was aided by a series of recorded audio interviews of Lew Rudin conducted by Louise Bobrow in 2001. (Audio recordings of these interviews were provided to the author by the Association for a Better New York.) Rudin spoke about his father's and grandfather's "gut feeling" for the real estate business. Also, Jack Rudin discussed his family history with Jack Emmerling in the video *The Rudin Family of New York: Featuring Jack Rudin.*
4. Lew Rudin, audio interview by Louise Bobrow, 2001
5. Jack Bigel, transcript of interview conducted for the documentary video *The Lew Rudin Way* (New York: 2006) DVD, Jan, 9, 2002. Transcripts of this and other interviews conducted for the documentary were provided to the author by the Association for a Better New York.
6. Lew Rudin, Brobrow interview.
7. Wolfgang Saxon, "May Rudin, Philanthropist and Real Estate Owner," *New York Times,* July 24, 1992.
8. Lewis Rudin interviewed by Bobrow, 2001.
9. Ibid.
10. Jack Rudin, Emmerling interview.
11. Ibid.

12. Ibid.
13. Bill Rudin, interview.
14. Kenneth Langone, telephone interview by the author, May 20, 2013.
15. Bill Rudin, interview.

3. Entree to Politics and Policy

1. Alton Marshall, transcript of interview conducted for the documentary video *The Lew Rudin Way*, Dec. 17, 2002.
2. Marshall, interview.
3. Bagli, "Lewis Rudin, Head of Real Estate Family."
4. Jack Rudin, Emmerling interview
5. Howard Rubenstein, interview by the author, New York, NY, Oct. 10, 2012.
6. Beth Rudin DeWoody, interview by the author, New York, NY, Jan. 28, 2013.
7. Pamela Delaney, telephone interview by Robert Polner, Oct. 26, 2012.
8. Gotbaum, interview; Lew Rudin, Bobrow interview.
9. Mary Holloway, interview by the author, New York, NY, Dec. 31, 2012.
10. Koch, interview.
11. Bill Rudin, interview.
12. Ulam, Alex, "Lewis Rudin: Hanging On In Jittery Times," *The Real Deal,* April, 2008.
13. Lew Rudin, transcript of radio news interview, *John Wingate Show,* WOR-AM, April 15, 1974 (Radio TV Reports Inc.), transcript provided by the Association for a Better New York.
14. Felix Rohatyn, interview by the author, New York, NY, Dec. 3, 2012.
15. Percy Sutton, transcript of interview conducted for the documentary video *The Lew Rudin Way*, March 13, 2002.
16. Marshall, interview.

17. Jan Morris, *Manhattan '45* (New York: Oxford University Press, 1987), 65–68.
18. Martin Bregman, interview with Robert Polner, New York, NY, Jan. 4, 2013.
19. Koch, interview.
20. Kriegel, interview.
21. Victor Gotbaum, transcript of interview conducted for the documentary video *The Lew Rudin Way*, Jan. 23, 2002.
22. Dr. O. Wayne Isom, transcript of interview conducted for the documentary video *The Lew Rudin Way*, Fall 2002.
23. Bill Rudin, interview.
24. Bagli, "Lewis Rudin, Head of Real Estate Family"

4. Birth of the Association for a Better New York

1. As observed by the author, who was a New York state senator at the time.
2. Krigel, interview.
3. Ibid.
4. Ibid.
5. Kim Moody, *From Welfare State to Real Estate: Regime Change in New York City, 1974 to the Present* (New York: The New Press, 2007), 24–27.
6. Ibid.
7. Lew Rudin, Brobrow interview.
8. Richard Reeves, "Business Group Planning Improvements in Midtown," *New York Times*, Feb. 10, 1971, 1:2.
9. Rubenstein, interview.
10. Reeves, "Business Group Planning Improvements."
11. Ibid.
12. Lew Rudin, transcript of television news interview, *New York Report* (Lester Smith, moderator; Don Singleton of the *New York Daily News*, guest reporter), WOR-TV, Sept. 17, 1972, transcript provided by the Association for a Better New York.
13. Bigel, interview.

14. Matilda Cuomo, transcript of interview conducted for the documentary video *The Lew Rudin Way*, Feb. 27, 2001.
15. George Lence, telephone interview by Robert Polner, Dec. 3, 2012.
16. Rohatyn, interview.

5. The Film and Television Industry Comes of Age in New York City

1. Vanessa Wong, "New York's Film Industry Starts Rolling Again," *Business Week,* Nov. 7, 2012.
2. Bregman, interview.

6. The Looming New York City Fiscal Crisis

1. Jonathan Soffer, *Ed Koch and the Rebuilding of New York City* (New York: Columbia University Press, 2010), 113–20.
2. Ibid.
3. John Zuccotti, interview the by author and Robert Polner, New York, NY, Oct. 15, 2012.

7. Prepayment of Property Taxes, and the Road Back to Prosperity

1. Gerald R. Ford, transcript of interview by Bill Rudin conducted for the documentary video *The Lew Rudin Way*.
2. Lew Rudin, Bobrow interview.
3. Rohatyn, interview.
4. Hugh L. Carey, transcript of interview conducted for the documentary video *The Lew Rudin Way*, Dec. 11, 2001.
5. Phillip L. Zweig, *Wriston: Walter Wriston, Citibank, and the Rise and Fall of American Financial Supremacy* (New York: Crown Publishers, 1996), 509.
6. Ibid., 507.
7. Walter Wriston, transcript of interview conducted for the documentary video *The Lew Rudin Way*, March 15, 2002.

8. Manfred Ohrenstein, interview by the author, New York, NY, May 15, 2013.
9. Barry Feinstein, transcript of interview conducted for the documentary video *The Lew Rudin Way*, Jan. 29, 2002.
10. Wriston, interview.
11. Marshall, interview.
12. Jonathan Mahler, *Ladies and Gentlemen, The Bronx is Burning: 1977, Baseball, Politics, and the Battle for the Soul of a City* (Picador; Farrah, Strauss and Giroux: New York: 2005), 227.
13. Lew Rudin, Bobrow interview.
14. "Lewis Rudin Gets an Honorary Title," *New York Times*, May 2, 1979, C16.

8. New York City Marathon

1. Percy Sutton, transcript of interview conducted for the documentary video *The Lew Rudin Way*, March 13, 2002.
2. Eric Rudin, transcript of interview conducted for the documentary video *The Lew Rudin Way*, May 1, 2006.
3. Rubenstein, interview.

9. International Tennis Becomes Synonymous with New York

1. George Gowen (former general counsel of the USTA), interview by Robert Polner, New York, NY, Sept. 19, 2012.
2. David Kenneth Specter, "A Stadium is Born," *Tennis Week,* Feb. 20, 1997. The stadium architect's comprehensive article on the project aptly described the late-1976 negotiations as follows: "The West Side Tennis Club wanted the USTA to pay to expand their antiquated stadium, build six indoor courts, remodel and expand their clubhouse. Plus, the Club wanted to share heavily in the profits. Its members voted to make this a 'take it or leave it' deal. To spend what was estimated to over $7 million for a two week event, coupled with no greater control of the tournament, was unacceptable to the USTA."

3. Specter, "A Stadium is Born."
4. Julia Vitullo Martin, "Developers Saved the U.S. Open," *New York Sun,* Aug. 26, 2003.
5. David N. Dinkins, interview by the author and Robert Polner, New York, NY, Nov. 19, 2012.
6. Jonathan Tisch, interview by the author, New York, NY, Oct. 3, 2012.
7. Koch, interview; Dinkins, interview.
8. *New York Sun,* Aug. 26. 2003.
9. Gowen, interview.

10. Protecting Local and State Tax Deductions

1. Albert R. Hunt, introduction to *Showdown at Gucci Gulch: Lawmakers, Lobbyists, and the Unlikely Triumph of Tax Reform* by Jeffrey H. Birnbaum and Alan S. Murray (New York: Random House, 1987) xii.
2. Kriegel, interview.
3. Ibid.
4. James D. Robinson III, transcript of interview conducted for the documentary video *The Lew Rudin Way*, March 19, 2002.
5. Kriegel, interview.
6. Birnbaum and Murray, *Showdown at Gucci Gulch,* 113–16.
7. Lewis Rudin, Bobrow interview.
8. Michael McKee, interview by Robert Polner, New York, NY, Jan. 18, 2013.
9. Beth Rudin DeWoody, telephone interview by the author, Jan. 28, 2013.

11. A Living Landmark

1. Ophelia Rudin, transcript of interview conducted for the documentary video *The Lew Rudin Way.*
2. Martin Berger, transcript of interview conducted for the documentary video *The Lew Rudin Way*, March 12, 2001.

3. Rubenstein, interview.
4. Randi Weingarten, address to the Association for a Better New York and subsequent interview by the author, New York, NY, April 30, 2013.
5. Michelle Adams, telephone interview by the author, April 25, 2013.
6. Rachel Rudin, telephone interview by the author, April 24, 2013.
7. Vicki Lurie, interview by the author, New York, NY, May 9, 2013.
8. Kenneth Langone, interview.
9. Beth Rudin DeWoody, interview.
10. Bill Rudin, interview.

Index

Actor's Equity, 59
Adams, Michelle, 100
"Adopt a Park" program, 54
AIDS crisis, 43, 44, 66
Allen, Woody, 58
American Federation of State, County and Municipal Employees, 42
American Federation of Teachers, 100
American Job Creation Act of 2004, 95
Anderson, Warren, 74
Arthur Ashe Stadium, 88, 89
Associated Builders and Owners of Greater New York, 48
Association for a Better New York (ABNY), 100
  "Adopt a Park" program, 54
  budget, 45
  bulletproof vests for police and, 36, 105*n8*
  business presence involvement with New York problems, 51
  continuation of, 101
  defense of New York City image by, 48
  doormen fighting crime effort by, 53
  early agenda, 50, 51
  founding, x, 8, 45, 46, 49, 50, 51
  growth of, 11
  interest in quality of life issues, 48
  "Labor Relations" effort, 54
  membership, 45, 48, 50
  monthy forums, 11
  moves to clean up Times Square, 54
  Operation Clean Sweep, 50, 52, 53
  promotion of construction for convention center, 51
  public/private partnerships through, 36
  Rudin's vision for, 45–55
  sees need to improve environment around city buildings, 49
  success of, 34
  willingness to help City Hall with initiatives, 47

Baker, Jim, 94
Bankruptcy threat, xii, 21, 61–76
Barclay, Lori, 10
Baruch College Steven L. Newman Real Estate Institute, 37, 38
Battery Park, 13
Beame, Abe, 38, 41, 57, 58, 59, 61, 62, 63, 64, 65, 66, 67, 70, 72, 74, 83

Benenson, Charles, 8, 50
Berger, Martin, 99
Berger, Steven, 67
Bigel, Jack, 18, 52, 53, 67, 76
Birnbaum, Jeffrey, 91
Blackout of 1977, 76
Bloomberg, Michael, 81, 89
Board of Estimate, 84, 86
Brady Handgun Violence Prevention Act (1993), x
Bregman, Martin, 58, 59
Bristol-Myers Squibb, 19
Bruno, Joseph, 96
Burke, Michael, 33
Bush, George H.W., 11, 23
Bush, George W., 11
Business Improvement Districts (BIDs), 37

Cantowitz, Joshua, 15
Carey, Hugh, xi, 39, 67, 69, 71, 72, 73, 74, 75
Carnegie Hall, 42
Carter, Jimmy, 77
Castle Clinton (Battery Park), 13
Catholic Church, 9, 10
Cavanagh, James, 66, 67
Central Park, 16, 24, 41, 82, 84
Central Park Conservancy, 37
Central Synagogue, 1, 3, 4, 5
Chase Manhattan Bank, 46
Cheney, Dick, 70
Citibank, 8, 73, 88
Citizens Budget Commission, 47
Citizens Crime Commission, 42
City Charter amendment, 72, 73
City University of New York, 17, 18, 70, 71
Clinton, Bill, ix–x, 5, 11, 93, 100
Clinton, Chelsea, x
Clinton, Hillary, 3, 100
Columbia University College of Physicians and Surgeons, 22
CompuServe, 27
Concorde jet, 78, 79
Con Edison, 73
Cooper Union, 23
Corruption, 36
Crime, 2, 33, 49, 66, 76
  issue in mayoral elections, 38
Cuomo, Andrew, 53
Cuomo, Mario, 38, 53, 93, 95
Cuomo, Matilda, 53

The Daily Show (television), 60
D'Amato, Alfonse, 91, 92
Deepdale Country Club, 6
Delaney, Pamela, 35, 36
DeLury, John, 52, 53
DeMilia, Sam, 34, 35
Democratic Party nominating convention (1976), 9
DeWitt Clinton High School (Bronx), 25, 38
DeWoody, Beth Rudin, 5, 11, 34, 97, 101
Dinkins, David, 10, 41, 88, 89
Dog Day Afternoon (film), 58
Dolan, Timothy Cardinal, 10
Dole, Bob, 11
"Don't Be a Litter Bug" campaign, 52
Downtown Alliance, 28
Downtown-Lower Manhattan Association, 47
Drexel Burnham Lambert, 27
Drugs, 66, 93
Du Brul, Paul, 41

Economic Development Administration (EDA), 46

Economic Development Council of New York City (EDC), 46
Egan, Edward Cardinal, 10
Ellis Island, 13
Esposito, Meade, 35

Federal Aid to Education legislation, xi
Federation of Jewish Philanthropies of New York, 42
Feinstein, Barry, 75, 76
Film and television industry, 40, 57–60
  U.S. Open, 88, 90
First National City Bank, 73
Ford, Gerald, 10, 11, 93
  initially withholds support for New York City, 69, 70, 74
  National Press Club appearance, 70
  signs loan bill for New York City, 75
Francis, Clarence, 45

Gay Men's Health Crisis (GMHC), 43, 44
General Foods, 45
Giscard d'Estaing, Valery, 75, 78
Giuliani, Rudy, 27, 89
Goldin, Harrison J., 61, 66, 72
Goldman Sachs, 19
Goldmark, Peter, 67
Gore, Al, 11, 94
Gotbaum, Betsy, 9, 35, 105*n8*
Gotbaum, Victor, 35, 42
Gowen, George, 89, 90
Grand Central Terminal, 52
Great Depression, 17, 18
Gribetz, Judah, 67

Harlem Hospital Pediatrics Department, 22
Harris, Ira and Nicki, 100
Helmsley-Spear Inc., 50
The Help, 42
Hester, Slew, 85, 86, 87, 88, 89
Holloway, Mary, 35
Housing
  crisis, 38
  low and middle income, 41, 48, 64
  post-war shortages, 17, 64
Hunt, Albert R. 91
Hurricane Sandy, 81

IBM Corporation, 27
"I Love New York" slogan, 3
Immigration, 13, 14, 77
  liberalization of policies, 41–42
Immigration Law of 1965, 77
Incantation Children's Center, 22
"Information Technology Center," 27
International Red Cross, 24
Iona College, 23
Isom, O. Wayne, 43

Javits, Jacob, 92
Jewish Guild for the Blind, 24
Johnson, Lyndon, xi, 64, 77

Katzka, Gabriel, 58
Kemp, Jack, 11
Kennedy, Ted, 11
Kennedy Airport, 78
Kissinger, Henry, 10, 11
Kissinger, Louis, 10
Koch, Ed, 3, 9, 10, 36, 38, 41, 73, 89
Kolodner, Nathan, 43
Kriegel, Jay, 47, 48, 49, 92, 94

LaGuardia, Fiorello, 39
LaGuardia Airport, 40

Langone, Kenneth, 28, 101
Law & Order (television), 60
Lence, George, 53, 54
Lenox Hill Hospital, 42
"Lew Rudin Way," 7
The Lew Rudin Way (film), 70
The Lighthouse, 24
Lincoln Center, 22, 40, 42
Lindsay, John, 46, 47, 50, 52, 65, 67
Louis Armstrong Stadium, 86
Lower East Side, 13
  Chrystie Street, 14
  Valozhin Synagogue, 16
Lower Manhattan business district, 27, 28
Lurie, Vicki, 101

Marshall, Alton, 31, 32, 39, 50, 51, 76
Martin, Julia Vitullo, 90
Mayor's Office of Film, Theatre & Broadcasting, 60
McKee, Michael, 96, 97
Meals on Wheels, 42
Meese, Edwin, 95
Memorial Sloan-Kettering Center, 22
Mentoring USA, 42
Metropolitan Museum of Art, 22
Midler, Bette, 58
Minnelli, Liza, 58
Mitchell, George, 94
Modell, Art and Pat, 100
Municipal Assistance Corporation, 72
Murray, Alan, 91
Museum of Natural History, 22, 24
Myerson, Bess, 76

National Football League, 19
National Press Club, 70
Newfield, Jack, 41
New York Bank for Savings, 73
New York Chamber of Commerce, 46
New York City
  affordability to middle income citizens, 96
  banking boycott on City debt paper, 68
  bankruptcy threat, xii, 21, 61–76
  crime in, 2, 33, 38
  crumbling infrastructure in, 38
  declining conditions in, 33
  fiscal crises in, 2, 8, 39, 49, 61–76
  hopes for federal and state funding to stave off bankruptcy, 63, 66, 69
  layoffs of public employees in, 75
  loss of large companies to suburbs, 32, 33, 45, 46, 50
  municipal bond market in, 62–63
  1950s
    automated technology pushes shipping industry out, 64
    dwindling of economic activity in Port of NY, 64
    loss of large companies to suburbs, 32, 33, 46
    specialized manufacturing moves South/Southwest, 64
  1960s
    initiation of commuter tax, 46
    loss of large companies to suburbs, 32, 33, 46
  1970s
    banking boycott on New York City debt paper, 68, 71
    budget deficits, 66
    complaints to real estate leaders from commercial tenants

about business climate, 47
crime as electoral issue, 38
cutbacks in municipal services in, 66
exodus of businesses and population, 66
financial crises, 2, 8, 39, 49, 61–68
fiscal improvisations during, 74, 75
housing crisis, 38
imposition of fiscal control board, 75
infrastructure deficiencies, 38
layoffs of public employees in, 75
loss of Fortune 500 companies, 49
"New York is a Great College Town" promotion, 3
procurement of bulletproof vests for police, 9, 10, 34–37, 105n8
recession in, 38, 64, 65
renovation of Yankee Stadium, 34
restructuring of city debt, 75
threat of bankruptcy in, 69–76
welfare increases, 38
1980s
AIDS crisis, 43, 44
middle class residents desert city for suburbs, 49
"New York is a Great College Town" promotion, 3
1990s
elimination of commuter tax, 46
real estate crash, 27
over-borrowing in, 65
post-war housing shortage, 17, 64
property tax revenues in, 8
recession and inflation in, 64
school issues, 2, 38
seen as nation's cultural and financial capital, 77
state support to prevent default, 69
U.S. Open major revenue sources and, 87, 88, 89, 90
New York City Board of Education, xi
New York City Convention and Visitors Bureau, 50
New York City Industrial Development Bonds, 89
New York City Marathon, 40, 41, 81–84
New York City Office of Film and Television Production, 59, 60
New York City Partnership, 42, 46
New York City Planning Commission, 67
New York City Police Foundation, 9, 34, 35, 36, 42, 105*n8*
New York Daily News, 70, 72
"New York is a Great College Town," 3
New York Life Insurance, 73
New York (magazine), 6
New York Merchandise Mart, 21
New York Mets, 90
New York Post, 81
New York Road Runners Club, 82, 83
New York Sun, 90
New York Telephone, 73
New York Times, 12, 33, 50, 81
New York University, 8, 22, 25, 26, 38, 42
New York Yankees, 33, 90

Nixon, Richard, 10, 64
Nizer, Louis, 35
Nyman, Jack, 37, 38

O'Connor, John Cardinal, 10
O'Dwyer, Paul, 72
O'Dwyer, William, 10
Ohrenstein, Manfred, 74
Oil embargo, 64
Ollman, Bertell, 8
One World Trade Center, 101
Operation Clean Sweep, 50, 52, 53

Packwood, Bob, 92
PACT (Provide Addict Care Today) program, 54
Paprin, Maurice, 48
Partnership for New York City, 46
Pataki, George, 6
Patrolmen's Benevolent Association, 34, 35, 105*n8*
Philanthropy. *See* Public/private/non-profit projects
Phoenix House, 22
P.J. Clarke's (pub), 11
Poitier, Sidney, 6
Pollack, Milton, 79
Port Authority of New York, 78, 79
Powell, Colin, 11
PS 166 (West 89th Street), 24
Public/private/non-profit projects. *See also* Association for a Better New York (ABNY)
  bulletproof vests for police, 9, 10, 34–37, 105*n8*
  Business Improvement Districts, 37
  Central Park Conservancy, 37
  Citizens Crime Commission, 42
  Economic Development Council of New York City, 46
  Federation of Jewish Philanthropies of New York, 42
  Friends of the High Line, 37
  Gay Men's Health Crisis (GMHC), 43, 44
  Lincoln Center Theater, 42
  Meals on Wheels, 42
  Mentoring USA, 42
  National Tennis Center, 85–90
  New York City Partnership, 42, 46
  New York City Police Foundation, 42
  Partnership for New York City, 46
  Prospect Park Alliance, 37

Race
  barriers, 64
  riots, 2
  tensions, 2, 47
Ravitch, Richard, 67
Reagan, Ronald, ix, 11, 70, 91, 93, 95, 96
Reagan Library, 95
The Real Deal (magazine), 37
Real estate
  assessments on properties, 49, 65
  bubble, 96
  building abandonment, 49, 65
  crash of 1990s, 27
  evictions and, 96, 97
  first Rudin family interest in, 15, 16, 17
  growth of Rudin firm, 17–22
  increases in commercial rents, 31, 32
  informal arbitration panel for business owners facing rent increases, 32

lack of availability of office space, 31
loss of commercial/residential demand, 33
property taxes, 8, 9
re-zoning, 28
shortage of new development in, 31
Real Estate Board of New York, 48, 50
Recessions, 2, 38, 64, 65
Regan, Donald, 93, 95
Regency Hotel, 10
Regional Planning Association, 48
Rent
control, 8, 31, 32, 96
regulations, 48, 96
stabilization, 97
Roberts, Burton, 100
Robinson, James, 92, 94
Rockefeller, David, 20, 46, 47, 95
Rockefeller, John D., 14, 15
Rockefeller, Nelson, 20, 31, 39, 50, 74
Rockefeller Center, 21, 39, 50
Rohatyn, Felix, 39, 55, 67, 73, 76
Rostenkowski, Dan, 92, 93
Rubinstein, Howard, 8, 9, 34, 50, 52, 71, 83, 84, 100
Rudin, Bill, 3, 23, 34, 37, 101
Association for a Better New York (ABNY) and, 8
in family philanthropic foundations, 5
in Rudin Management Company, Inc., 26, 44
succeeds father, 100
Rudin, Eric, 26, 83, 101
Rudin, Gladyce, 11
Rudin, Jack, 10, 23, 34, 101
devotion to parents, 18
joins family real estate business, 26
liberalization of immigration policies and, 41–42
military service, 18, 25, 26
role in creating Jazz at Lincoln Center, 40
school years, 24
support for low and middle income housing, 41
work with civil service unions for retirement security, 41
Rudin, Lew
acquires bulletproof vests for police, 9, 10, 34–37, 105*n8*
assistance in keeping New York City from fiscal default, 61–68, 71–76
Association for a Better New York (ABNY) and, x, 8, 45–55
belief in public-private partnerships, 7, 34–37, 36, 37, 40–44
brings together former/current elected officials, 11
at City College, 17, 18
commitment to Israel, 5
death of, 1, 3, 4, 100
devotion to parents, 18, 20, 23
difficulties with glaucoma, 3, 99
efforts to keep United States Tennis Association in New York, 41, 85–90
as face of NYC real estate sector, 8
family history, 13–29
help for film and television industry, 40, 57–60
honorary chairman of New York City Marathon, 83
"I Love New York" slogan and, 3

Rudin, Lew *(continued)*
joins family real estate business, 26
learns importance of personal contact with those in power, 32, 58, 59, 100
liberalization of immigration policies and, 41–42
made honorary Officer of the Most Excellent Order of the British Empire (OBE), 79
military service, 18, 25
moves to clean up Times Square, 54
negotiating ability, 4
"New York is a Great College Town" banner, 3
as New York's unofficial ambassador, 76
in Operation Clean Sweep, 50, 52, 53
opposes real estate price controls, 31
PACT (Provide Addict Care Today) program and, 54
personalized manner of doing business, 8
philanthropic foundations, 5, 22, 23, 42–44
in policymaking and politics, 31–44
preventing elimination of federal tax deductions for state/local taxes, 41, 91–98
promotes "burden sharing," 75, 76
provision of rentals to retired government officials, 10
pushes owners to pre-pay property taxes, 8, 9, 72–79
reacts against suspected slights against New York City, 12
reinvention of New York City Marathon by, 40, 41, 81–84
on rent control/stabilization, 8
revival of Lincoln Center and, 40
school years, 24
seeks to strengthen city's reputation as business destination, 77, 78
sincerity in desire to help, 53
support for education, 22, 23
support for low and middle income housing, 41
at Townsend Harris High School, 17
treatment of people from all stations of life, 4, 28, 29
view on philanthropy as lever of civic improvement, 42
wide range of acquaintances, ix, 9
work with civil service unions for retirement security, 41
Rudin, May, 17, 22, 23, 24
Rudin, Michael, 6, 101
Rudin, Ophelia, 99
Rudin, Rachel, 3, 23, 100
Rudin, Sam, 10, 14, 16, 17, 27, 38, 83
Rudin, Samantha, 23, 101
Rudin, Susan, 10
Rudin family
determination to persevere in bad business climates, 27
early businesses, 14, 15
first real estate interests, 15, 16, 17
founds management company, 16
immigration from Eastern Europe, 13, 14
net worth, 27
philanthropic activities, 22, 23, 42–44

support for education, 22, 23
weathers Great Depression, 17, 18
Rudin Management Company, Inc., 73
1 Battery Park Plaza, 19
115 West Eighty-Sixth Street, 17, 24
commercial holdings, 16, 19, 21, 28
conversions to smart buildings, 27
80 Pine Street, 19, 28
55 Broad Street, 19, 27
founding, 16
41 Madison Avenue, 19, 21
1400 Benson Street, 17
"Information Technology Center," 27
Lexington Avenue, 16, 19
New York Merchandise Mart, 21
residential holdings, 17, 24, 26
"Silicon Alley," 28
Third Avenue, 20
3 Times Square, 26
345 Park Avenue, 19, 101
295 Central Park West, 17, 26
Rudinsky, Harry, 13
Rudinsky, Joseph, 13, 15
Rudinsky, Louis, 13, 14, 15, 16, 104*n3*
Rudinsky, Rachel, 13, 16
Rumsfeld, Donald, 70
Russo, Martin, 93
R.W. Pressprich & Company, 28

St. Luke's-Roosevelt Medical Center, 22
St. Patrick's Cathedral, 10
Samuel and May Rudin Foundation, 22
Schmidt, Helmut, 75
Schneider, Irving, 8, 50, 52
Schools, public
antiquated schools, 38
decentralization of, xi
overcrowding, 2
Schumer, Charles, 93
Serpico (film), 58
Sex and the City (television), 60
Shea Stadium, 87
"Silicon Alley," 28
Simon, William, 70, 74
"Singer Bowl," 86
Specter, David Kenneth, 86, 87, 108*n2*
Spellman, Francis Joseph Cardinal, 10
Spitz, George, 82
Streisand, Barbra, 58
Strikes
labor, 47
sanitation workers, 97
subway, 47
teachers, xi
Subways
aging, 33
fare increases, 76
filming in, 57
strikes, 47
Sun Microsystems, 27
Sutton, Percy, 39, 82, 83
Swan, Bill, 52

The Taking of Pelham One Two Three (1974 film), 57, 58, 59
Tax(es)
commuter, 46
corporate, 91
credits for construction of low and middle income housing, 41
credits to film companies, 59, 60
deductions, ix, 41, 42, 91–98
delinquencies in, 65
depreciation schedule and, 95
income, 94

Tax(es) *(continued)*
  individual rates, 94
  loopholes, 93, 97
  opposition to, 65
  prepayment of, 8, 9, 72–79
  property, 8, 65
  reform initiatives, 91, 92, 93
  restraint on growth of, 49, 65
  revenue shortfalls, 65
  sales, 95
  shelters, 94
  state, 98
  state/local income, ix, 41
  Tax Reform Act of 1986 and, 94
  trickle-down policies, 96
Teachers strikes, xi
Teamsters Union, 59
Tenant advocacy, 96, 97
Tennis Week (magazine), 87
Terrorist attack, 1, 6, 82, 101, 102
Throgs Neck, 17
Times Square, 54
Tisch, Jonathan, 89
Tisch, Preston Robert, 8, 50, 52
Tishman, Alan V., 50
Tishman Realty, 50
Tompkins, Rexford, 8, 50, 51
Tourism, 2, 40, 48, 52, 97
Townsend Harris High School, 17
Truman, Harry, 25

Unemployment, 64
United Federation of Teachers, 100
United States Tennis Association (USTA), 41, 85–90, 108*n2*
Urban decline, 2
U.S. House Ways and Means Committee, 92, 93
U.S. Open Tennis, 85–90
U.S. Senate Finance Committee, 92

Valozhin (Russian Empire), 14
Valozhin Synagogue, 16
Van Arsdale, Harry, 95
Vests, bulletproof, 9, 10, 34–37, 105*n8*
Violence, gun, 36
Violent Crime Control and Law Enforcement Act (1994), x

Wagner, Robert, 65
Wall Street, 19, 20, 28, 40, 96
Wall Street Journal, 71
Weingarten, Randi, 100
West Side Highway, 62
West Side Tennis Club, 85, 86, 108*n2*
Westway, 78
Whalen, Grover, 39, 40
White House (Washington, D.C.), 23
Wingate, John, 38
World's Fair (1964), 86
World Trade Center, 1, 82. *See also* Terrorist attacks
World War II, 18, 24, 25
  need for housing after, 17, 64
  return of servicemen to New York City after, 63, 64
Wriston, Walter, 8, 73, 74, 75

Zuccotti, John, 67